GOLFING
WITH YOUR EYES
CLOSED

GOLFING
WITH YOUR EYES
CLOSED

Mastering Visualization Techniques for Exceptional Golf

■

ERIN MACY AND **TIFFANY WILDING-WHITE**

New York Chicago San Francisco Lisbon London Madrid Mexico City
Milan New Delhi San Juan Seoul Singapore Sydney Toronto

Library of Congress Cataloging-in-Publication Data

Macy, Erin.
    Golfing with your eyes closed : mastering visualization techniques for exceptional
golf / Erin Macy and Tiffany Wilding-White.
        p.   cm.
    Includes bibliographical references and index.
    ISBN-13: 978-0-07-161507-5 (alk. paper)
    ISBN-10: 0-07-161507-5 (alk. paper)
    1. Golf—Psychological aspects.   2. Visualization.   I. Wilding-White,
Tiffany.   II. Title.

    GV979.P75M335   2009
    796.352—dc22   2008038135

1 2 3 4 5 6 7 8 9 10 11 12 13 14 15 16 17 18 19 20 21 22   FGR/FGR 0 9

ISBN 978-0-07-161507-5
MHID   0-07-161507-5

Interior design by Think Design Group LLC
Interior photographs for chapters 1, 6, and 7 by John Macy. Interior photographs for
chapters 4, 5, 8, and 9 by Erin Macy. Interior photograph for chapter 2 by Eric King. Interior
photograph for chapter 3 by Gary Allen.

McGraw-Hill books are available at special quantity discounts to use as premiums and
sales promotions or for use in corporate training programs. To contact a representative,
please visit the Contact Us pages at www.mhprofessional.com.

This book is printed on acid-free paper.

*To John. Thank you for your unconditional
commitment and confidence in me.*
—E.M.

*To Mom and Dad, for sharing with me
the love of life.
And to Carter, the love of my life.*
—T.W.

CONTENTS

ACKNOWLEDGMENTS

n writing *Golfing with Your Eyes Closed: Mastering Visualization Techniques for Exceptional Golf*, we appreciate the enthusiasm, expertise, and editing shared by those close to us. Thank you to our most amazing and supportive husbands, John and Carter, who are also our biggest fans.

Our thanks go to those whose expertise in golf contributed to the writing of this book: Michael Greller, Tom Greller, MaryJo McCloskey, Tim Hyatt, Matt Beck, Christine Collier, and Rob and Melissa O'Neill. To our editor, Ron Martirano, for his belief in our project, and to Alexis Hurley for her time and professional insight. Many others gave valued advice along the way: Dr. Dan Benardot, Lori Blair, Madeleine Blais, Michelle Choy, Dr. Keith Henschen, and Dan McCracken.

To our incredible editing team: Sherry Macy, Vicki Sanders, and Debby and Bill Winslow. It's in the genes.

To our classmates Amy, Brian, Chris, and Dan, who were part of the original project and to Dr. Greg Shelley for the initial inspiration. George Fox University was generous to provide many of the photos sprinkled throughout the book.

Through it all, we are thankful for our friends, especially Julie and the Newberg family, for their interest and cheerleading in what we've been working to complete. And always, to our families, for their constant love, encouragement, and positive influence in our lives.

AN INTRODUCTION TO THE FIFTEENTH CLUB

The Path to Peak Performance

Success in golf depends less on strength of body than upon strength of mind and character.

—ARNOLD PALMER[1]

Trophies, titles, new records, personal bests, satisfaction, and strong social relationships—nearly every athlete strives for these. In this book, we give you the keys to mental success in golf. Certainly, real success requires a good handle on both your physical and mental game. No one gets very far without a light grip, balanced stance, and mastery of basic swing mechanics, but we're leaving the physical aspects up to you and your golf instructor. The mental skills—the so-called fifteenth club that most players and experts know constitutes more than 80 percent of the game—are all in here. The trick is to combine your physical prowess with mental imagery. This powerful duo can take you to new heights in performance.

We have written *Golfing with Your Eyes Closed* as a mental training program for golfers of all levels. The material can easily be applied by everyone, from beginners to scratch golfers to pros. The wording is straightforward and casual, making it fun and simple to understand. At whatever level you play golf, learning to add or refine mental imagery and visualization to your game will help you reach your peak performance.

Our aim in creating *Golfing with Your Eyes Closed* is to provide you with complete information on what it takes to consistently play the best golf you can on the course. We hope you will gain new and useful information from this book and then implement what you learn the very next time you tee off. While you probably have already heard something about the effectiveness of mental imagery, you will find the detailed how-to here in this book. It offers exercises for you to try, key points to remember, a series of tips for coaches and players, and anecdotes as well as personal advice from instructors and players. You'll meet Christine, a National Collegiate Athletic Association (NCAA) golfer who has learned to refocus after missing a shot. You'll meet Matt and Mary Jo, collegiate coaches who develop leaders on their golf teams. We'll introduce you to avid golfers Tom, Michael, and Tim, who are always looking for ways to take their game to the next level, and to Bill, a retired businessman whose positive-thinking skills help him on and off the course. How do we know it will work? Because the difference between two equally well-trained players draining the putt or lipping out lies in the strength of their mental control.

Visualization, or imagery, as we also call it, is the equivalent of playing movies in your head. You can see, feel, hear, and even smell and taste the elements of the perfect round of golf. Time and again, you'll observe high-level players using mental rehearsal to increase their confidence, sharpen their concentration, control their nerves, and strengthen their motivation. Mental imagery is one of the most powerful tools for performance enhancement. By experiencing your performance in your mind, you can see marked improvement in your performance on the course. With training and practice, you can master this mental skill and implement it easily and consistently.

Visualization has numerous applications: it can be used to prevent errors, correct mistakes, enhance consistency, strengthen muscle memory, assess and perfect your swing's appearance and feeling, calm and energize, encourage healing, and promote success. Imagery can be highly beneficial. So how do you get good at it?

By following this book, you will:

→ assess your current imagery patterns
→ learn the benefits and uses of imagery
→ understand the theories behind why visualization works
→ practice imagery to feel how it affects your muscle memory
→ learn how to consistently turn nervous energy into positive performances
→ concentrate and avoid choking under pressure
→ refocus after a concentration lapse and between shots
→ identify what motivates you
→ establish a M.A.S.T.E.R. goal-setting program to build golf-specific motivation
→ create your own personal goal achievement plan to help you realize your golf ambitions

→ discover how to develop a consistently positive mind-set
→ design your own personal imagery routines and scripts
→ apply your new mental skills on and off the course
→ assess your progress, and create concrete and attainable plans for continued improvement in golf

Imagine—you're just steps away from playing a better game of golf!

What separates the best of us from the rest of us? Mental sharpness. Reading and implementing the exercises in *Golfing with Your Eyes Closed* can pave the path to your peak performance. We provide the keys; you provide the drive. Champions go to sleep at night visualizing their best performances, and they wake up determined to turn their visions into reality. By practicing mental imagery, you can be a champion in your golf game, too.

SELF-ASSESSMENT SCORECARD

The first step in being able to "golf with your eyes closed" is to determine how you use visualization, the strength of your mental muscle, and where you will most benefit from learning some new skills. You may never have used visualization before. Maybe you visualize by following an imaginary ball along its path to your target. Or you may try to visualize during tournament play. Regardless of your experience, take time to answer the self-assessment questions that follow. Doing so will give you a baseline by which you can measure your improvement as you learn how to visualize and begin to practice.

Imagine that each question is set up as a par-three hole. Assign a number value for your answers according to the provided scale, marking answers to questions 1–18 in the initial assessment line of the Self-Assessment Scorecard on page xvi. These questions and your responses will be referred to throughout the book.

1 = Consistently (eagle)
2 = Mostly (birdie)
3 = Sometimes (par)
4 = Rarely (bogey)
5 = Never (double bogey)

1. I visualize on the driving range and while at home or work.
2. I visualize my shots before and during a round of golf.

3. In my imagery, I see myself performing from an outside perspective, as if through a video camera (externally).
4. In my imagery, I see myself performing from my own viewpoint (internally).
5. The colors and visual surroundings of my images are clear and detailed.
6. The sounds during my performance are sharp and audible in my mental rehearsal.
7. I can change my images in my mind to reflect my desired performance.
8. I use a pre-shot routine when I take a full shot.
9. When playing golf, I am positive and in control of my emotions.
10. I am confident with each shot I take.
11. I effectively shut out negative thoughts.
12. I play well under pressure.
13. After every shot, I am able to mentally leave behind whatever I just did and begin to focus fully on my next shot.
14. To help me concentrate and avoid choking, I use relaxation techniques like visualization and deep breathing.
15. It's easy for me to relax between shots and then to regain my focus as needed.
16. I have very specific goals for golf and a detailed plan to achieve them.
17. The main reason I play is for pure enjoyment, not for rewards like money, fame, or business gains.
18. Both on the course and off, I find myself visualizing many different scenarios, from school or business to public speaking or other performances.

Questions 19–24 assess your general visualization, motivation, concentration, and confidence patterns. Write your responses in the area provided.

19. If you have ever visualized, when did you do it? (At night? During your trip to the course? Before every shot?) Note how consistent you are.

_____

_____

_____

_____

_____

_____

20. Where can you image most clearly? (While lying in bed with your eyes closed? At the range? At a particular hole on your home course?)

_____

_____

_____

_____

_____

_____

21. Do you usually visualize an entire round, from shot to shot, in order, and all the way through? Or just some key elements? Describe the scenes you usually visualize.

_____

_____

_____

_____

_____

22. In which circumstances do you feel most affected by nerves?

_____

_____

_____

_____

23. Imagine that you're cursing over a bad shot or thinking about what you're going to do after the round. In such a case, what would you usually do to bring your focus back to the present shot?

_____

_____

_____

_____

_____

_____

24. Which specific parts of your game are you hoping to improve by completing the exercises in this golfer's mental training guide?

_____

_____

_____

_____

_____

_____

Golfing with Your Eyes Closed Self-Assessment Scorecard																			
QUESTION	1	2	3	4	5	6	7	8	9	10	11	12	13	14	15	16	17	18	TOT
PAR	3	3	3	3	3	3	3	3	3	3	3	3	3	3	3	3	3	3	54
INITIAL ASSESSMENT																			
1 MONTH																			
2 MONTHS																			
3 MONTHS																			
6 MONTHS																			
9 MONTHS																			
1 YEAR																			
SCORER:																			

Add up your scores from questions 1–18 on the Self-Assessment Scorecard. If your totals were:

→ **66–90:** As a newcomer to visual mental training techniques, you will notice a significant improvement in performance by incorporating the basic lessons of *Golfing with Your Eyes Closed* into your game on a regular basis. Visualization is a skill that takes practice, so let's get going! Don't be overwhelmed by everything you read here. Take it one step at a time, and make sure you really understand each concept before moving onto the next one. There's no need to rush—just like in your golf game, it's important to take the time to line up your mental shots. With patience and practice, you will definitely see improvements in your ability to visualize on the course.

→ **37–65:** Having experience in visualization, you should find your game becoming more consistent as you learn to visualize consistently. By implementing the exercises presented throughout, you'll enjoy the game more and lower your score as you play. As you find areas where you are not as strong, take extra care to complete all the exercises and to integrate the visualization training tips into your game.

→ **18–36:** As a skilled visualizer, you may have a pretty good handle on visualization and its usefulness in performance enhancement. But there's always room for improvement. Within this book, you'll find effective methods to hone and sharpen your mental skills to take your game to a higher level. Each exercise is adaptable to your level of mental and physical ability. Even tour players constantly seek out different exercises to help advance their mental play.

As you read through the chapters, we'll touch on these questions again. Keep your answers close at hand for easy reference. Once you are finished with the book and have begun implementing our advice, use the Self-Assessment Scorecard periodically to evaluate improvements in your visualization ability as you put into practice the methods and instruction from this book.

GOLFING
WITH YOUR EYES
CLOSED

1

Your Ace
in the Hole

Michael is an amateur golfer whose mind often gets the better of him in the game. He has had a difficult summer on the course, losing to his rivals nearly every round. Often, it takes just one mistake to break his rhythm, leading to more mental errors and missed shots.

Michael knows the value of visualization and has tried off and on to implement it in his game. As an important tournament approaches, he begins to practice it more consistently, seeing each stroke in his mind's eye before he makes it. At home, off the course, he pictures himself at the tournament and in a variety of situations on each hole.

The day of the tournament arrives, and Michael is feeling confident, believing in his ability to be near the top of the leaderboard. He arrives at the course at his usual forty-five minutes ahead of time and runs through his warm-up routine. Ready but anxious, Michael steps into the first tee box, going through the motions he has practiced so many times. He drives through the ball. It carries over a small ridge and comes to rest on the fairway. He's off to a great start! His approach shot lands him on the green within range for a sinkable putt, and he is feeling good. He lines up for an easy putt and blows it five feet past the hole. Frustrated, Michael uses an extra minute to collect himself, taking the time to go through his visualization routine and even seeing his name on the leaderboard. He addresses the ball for his second putt, repeating his mental mantra to himself. Body balanced, he gently strikes the ball. He hears the ball hit the bottom of the cup, and his confidence returns.

TEEING OFF

In your own golf game, you've probably felt the frustration of blowing an easy putt and wondered, "How could I have missed that?" Logic tells you that your lineup was accurate, your read of the green was right on, and your stroke was smooth. But reality shows that something went awry. Most likely, it was your mental composure. Like Michael in the previous example, you may have rushed a little instead of slowly taking each step in your pre-shot routine. By learning to visualize, you increase the likelihood of making more shots more regularly, because you become sharply focused on the exact actions required to consistently hit your target.

This first chapter introduces you to the basics of visualization and gets you started on a plan of action. The theories, examples, and exercises here help you:

→ understand the different forms of visualization
→ practice both external and internal imagery at appropriate times
→ focus on the positive images and block out negative pictures
→ keep in mind the theories that govern visualization's power over your game
→ replace thinking with visualization on the course
→ integrate the elements that make images come to life

You may want to consider the exercises that follow in this chapter to be as important as your pregame preparations. You wouldn't play golf without first taking out your clubs, tying your golf shoes, and putting on your glove. This chapter, like those rituals, is both basic and essential to playing your best.

IMAGERY'S INNER WORKINGS

In the movie *The Greatest Game Ever Played*, two different styles of visualization are portrayed. Harry Vardon brilliantly erases every distraction surrounding him—the crowd, the noise, and even the trees lining the fairway. He wipes these images out and sees only his target. Francis Ouimet, on the other hand, creates a picture of the hole being extremely large by making his mind zoom in and fixing his aim on this one point.[1] Other players use different techniques. Jack Nicklaus talked about seeing the shot take form before he even addressed the ball, and Sam Snead compared visualization to painting a picture of the shot he planned to hit.[2] Imagery comes in many forms, and this section should help you determine the most beneficial form for *your* golf game.

Forms of Visualization

Visualization can be external or internal. If you practice visualizing externally, you see yourself from an observer's view, as if watching a video of your performance. Visualizing internally, you see yourself executing a skill through your own eyes— what you actually see when performing. For example, a golfer visualizing herself

I never hit a shot, not even in practice, without having a very sharp, in-focus picture of it in my head. First I see the ball where I want it to finish, nice and white and sitting up high on the bright green grass. Then the scene quickly changes, and I see the ball going there: its path, trajectory, and shape, even its behavior on landing. Then there is a sort of fade-out, and the next scene shows me making the kind of swing that will turn the previous images into reality.

—*JACK NICKLAUS*[3]

teeing off from an external perspective sees her feet shoulder-width apart; arms, chest, and hands coming together to form a triangle; her head tilted at an angle; and her eyes focusing on the ball. From an internal perspective, however, she only sees the tee and the ball, the grass underfoot, her feet, and in her peripheral vision she may see the natural surroundings of the course.

Your answers to questions 3 and 4 of the Self-Assessment Scorecard show you how you visualize.

COACH'S CORNER

Try this exercise to help your players learn the power of imagery: Tie a weight to the end of a string six to twelve inches long. Have them hold the end of the string, close their eyes, and keep their hand and arm perfectly still. Ask them to visualize the string and weight swinging like a pendulum, back and forth, back and forth. Lead them through this for about one minute. When they open their eyes, the string will actually be swinging, convincing them of the strength of their mind-body connection. This should really wow them!

External visualization is used to assess how a stroke looks to an observer. It allows you to analyze your body positions, thereby enabling you to correct mistakes and refine your movements. On the other hand, internal imagery is used to assess how your swing feels. Repeatedly visualizing from your own perspective helps internalize the feeling of a stellar performance. Once you can see and feel your mistakes or fears, you can correct them by mentally rehearsing the right technique instead. Regularly creating images of the performance you hope to achieve equips you to execute under pressure.

Try it! Let's imagine the same scene from two different viewpoints. First, close your eyes and visualize externally: You stand on the green, alone, wearing a collared shirt and pants and carrying your putter. Other golfers watch you from the edge of the green. They are completely silent as you take your time examining the green and lining up your putt. You approach the ball, align your body, and take a practice swing. Take your normal stance and address the ball. Like a pendulum, your arms swing and you strike the ball. Watch the ball travel across the green and drop into the hole.

Now try visualizing this same scene from your own internal perspective.

Notice the differences. From an external perspective, you probably saw the other golfers, your putter in your hands, and the contours of the green. From the internal perspective, you probably saw the ball and felt the putter extending from your arms. Make a note whether one form was easier for you than the other.

Given this information, you may ask, "So which one should I use?" The answer is both! A combination of the two perspectives is optimal. Continuing with the preceding example, the golfer putting on the green needs to use external visualization to see her tempo and follow through. She also needs to use internal imagery to experience what a correct putt feels like. With the two together, she can make corrections and perfect her putt.

The more time you spend practicing visualization, the easier it will be to quickly apply this skill on the golf course. While it might seem like a lot right now, you can visualize any shot in just a second or two—the same time it takes to make a practice swing. So don't get overwhelmed. Just take it one step at a time, and it will become second nature before you know it.

Most athletes are naturally more comfortable with one kind of visualization than the other and require practice to perfect both types. Some athletes, though, flip back and forth between the two without thinking. With only a few minutes of visualization practice each day, you can learn to control these images. Read on to find out how to apply this "mental video" to your game.

The Body Achieves What the Mind Believes

Now that you understand the two different forms of visualization, we can briefly discuss why imagery works. To start, know this: the body achieves what the mind believes. Thus you want to visualize positively.

For example, if we say, "Do *not* think of a bright purple golf ball," what do you think about? The purple ball, right? Yet if we say, "*Do* think of a purple golf ball," you still picture that same odd-colored ball. The trick is, your mind focuses only on the object or action, without distinguishing between the *do* or *don't*. So by stating your desires *positively*, you trigger your mind to focus on what you want rather than on what you don't want. By visualizing *only* positive images, you deny your brain the chance to latch on to negative images, and thus you promote peak performance. Think, "I'm going to hit a nice high cut into the center of the fairway," rather than, "Don't hit into the lake," or, "Try not to hit out of bounds." Picture yourself sinking the putt rather than thinking about avoiding hitting it four feet past the hole. Effectively, you can block out doubts, worries, and fears by visualizing positive images of performance.

What negative thoughts or images do you have when you perform? Example: "Don't leave this putt short."

1. _____

2. _____

3. _____

Which positive thoughts or images could you use instead? Example: "Give the putt a chance."

1. _____

2. _____

3. _____

Anytime you have a negative thought or picture yourself making a mistake, consciously replace that destructive thought or image with a positive one. If you worry that you might hit into a hazard, picture yourself striking the ball down the middle of the fairway.

The imagination principle also helps clarify why imagery works. It asserts that your mind cannot tell the difference between reality and imagination.[4] Therefore, you can condition your body to perform better through visualization, because your body physically reacts to imagined situations, as well as to real ones. As an example, have you ever been nearly asleep, dreamed you were falling off a cliff, and then jerked awake? Your mind did not know the difference between *dreaming* you were falling and *actually* falling. So by visualizing your performance skills— your stance, your grip, your backswing and follow-through—your mind believes you are actually performing, thereby building confidence and consistency.

In fact, the muscle memory theory indicates that during imagery, the muscles involved in the skills you visualize become slightly activated, duplicating the actual pattern that takes place during physical exercises.[5] Further evidence of this comes from a Harvard University study that shows that the brain processes both mental imagery and images we actually see in the same area of the brain.[6] Practicing imagery thus strengthens the mind-body connection and helps make golf performance more consistent.

To illustrate this, we know of an elite 800-meter runner who consistently runs his race in his head in exactly the time it takes him to run it in real life! His mental imagery is spot on; his mind and body connect so intimately that his mental rehearsal exactly duplicates his physical workout. In fact, during a laboratory test, sensors indicated his muscles actually activated parallel to what he pictured at that moment, while sitting down and visualizing. Specifically, his muscles tightened as he sped up and fired asymmetrically as he leaned into each turn.[7] Thus through visualization, he strengthens his muscle memory while sitting in a chair!

Also, 2005 world champion Laura Wilkinson used imagery to help her win an Olympic gold medal in platform diving. Months before the 2000 Sydney Games, her foot was in a cast. Unable to physically practice, she mentally rehearsed to perfect her dives. Her body was actually slightly physically activated during imagery, so it was ready as soon as her cast came off, and she gave the performance of her life.

When you become aware of how your mind and body work together, you begin to perform more fluidly and consistently. How do you gain awareness? By tuning in and paying attention to how each move feels. Focus on sights, sounds, and feelings, and practice mentally rehearsing these thoughts, sights, sounds, and feelings. The keener your awareness of these sensations, the more real and vivid you can make your images and the more effective they will be in improving your game.

Visualize yourself performing one stroke perfectly. Repeat this image again and again in your head. (You may need to slow down your mental video to gain control.) Take the time to focus on the senses of sight, sound, smell, and touch.

COACH'S CORNER

Be aware that you think differently than your players do. Coaches tend to analyze and instruct, as is your job. Your verbal comments come from the left side of your brain, the "thinker." However, athletes perform from their right brain, the "doer." Therefore, it would be helpful for you to give them instructions that stimulate their right brain, like imagery. Encouraging their creative mind allows them to stop thinking and start doing.

Also note that as players' anxiety increases, their left brain becomes dominant. So take care to keep them from becoming anxious, by incorporating relaxation. This way, they can operate from their right brain and not be hindered by the analytical left brain.

A Split Brain

Here's an interesting concept to remember: the left half of your brain concentrates on different aspects of performance than the right half does. Knowing the specifics helps you focus your energy in the appropriate areas. The left brain is the thinker—very logical and analytical. Conversely, the right brain is the doer and is creative. Performance is a right-brained activity. Your right brain is your body's autopilot, taking over and "just doing it."

Visualization requires creativity and therefore takes place in the right brain. Hence, by practicing imagery, your right brain becomes more familiar with just doing it and does not hesitate by thinking about it. Since thinking can get in the way of successful performance, using your creative right brain to image engages the doer in your mind and silences the thinker. Let visualization take the place of thinking.

The next time you find yourself overanalyzing each movement in your swing or facing a competitor who intimidates you, press "play" on your mental video to recall a previous right-brain performance. Visualize that experience; relive it in your mind. Note on the following lines how well these images effectively block out your doubts and fears and allow your body to perform without hesitation.

_____

_____

_____

_____

VIVACIOUS VISUALIZATION

Imagery should be vivid, controllable, and positive. It will take time and practice to make sure each element is part of your images, but keep working at it. The better your images, the stronger your mind and body will be linked.

By *vivid*, we mean that the images should be clear, intense, and full of detail. Use all of your senses to make your images as realistic as possible. Try to feel the temperature, smell the freshly cut grass, hear the sound the club makes as it strikes the ball, sense the way the club feels in your hands, or whatever it is that your senses notice. You want to be able to conjure up images with every detail present.

Controlling your images has two meanings. First, it refers to being able to manipulate speed, tempo, and direction. Maybe you want to slow down your swing

> Visualization lets you concentrate on all the positive aspects of your game.
>
> —CURTIS STRANGE [8]

in your mind and analyze your takeaway. Or maybe you have been rushing through your tee shots and want to visualize yourself taking your time to prepare. The second definition has to do with the responsibility you have to be in charge of what your images do. You direct your images; you choose how you want your swing to look, how you address the ball, the result of a shot, and even your emotional response. Aim for a state where you can get your images to do what you want. Maintain control of your mind, not allowing your images to turn into daydreams for which you are not actively responsible. Being able to modify your images and tell them to do what you want them to do is important. Take charge of your mind.

BEST MATCH: RELAX, DETACH

Christine

As Dr. Bob Rotella states, "Golf is not a game of perfect." However, it is my personality to make it one. I have learned over the years that golf is a game of misses. The best players know how to manage their misses and get out of trouble quickly to avoid the high numbers. Recently, I have been learning to allow myself to play well. It is so easy for me to get on a hot streak, but think in my mind, "I have to hold on to this," or even worse, "Oh no, it's only a matter of time before I screw up." These thoughts creep in, and before I know it, they have come true. Therefore, I must stay relaxed, mind and body, and allow myself to play well. My mind has to stay quiet for me to perform well. My golf coach has the best advice for this. She tells me to remain unattached to the shots. If I just hit the best shot of my life, I acknowledge the good act, but I do not get too excited about it. Instead I move on to the next one.

The same is true if I make a bad shot. I acknowledge it and move on as emotionally unattached as possible. If I hit the ball exactly where I wanted to every time, I would be the best player in the world, but that is not a reality. I have to accept the missed hits and recover from them as best as possible. It is easy for me to be overly critical of myself and lose confidence. What has helped me overcome this tendency has been to "act as if." I read this statement in a sport psychology book once, and it has really stuck with me. Why not pretend to be Tiger Woods out there? This is a form of visualization that is fun and has really worked for me. When I act as if I am the best golfer in the world, it brings me confidence and focus. I see myself pulling off great golf shots and fiercely competing. It changes my attitude from doubting to believing to ultimately achieving.

See Self-Assessment Scorecard questions 5–7 for your self-ratings on vividness and controllability.

Start incorporating vividness by picturing yourself completing a simple and familiar task. You might choose mowing the lawn, buttering a piece of toast and then eating it, answering the phone at work, putting your shoes on in the morning, sitting around a campfire with friends, or any number of scenarios. Take your time visualizing. Amplify your five senses, and become aware of how things smell, look, taste, feel, and sound.

Did you visualize this scene internally or externally? Go back and watch it the other way to get a sense of what it looks and feels like in each style. Practice seeing yourself completing the task from within and from the outside so you can easily use both methods to improve your performance.

After going through your imagery session, list what you noticed.

Sight: _____

Sound: _____

Smell: _____

Touch: _____

Taste: _____

Once you feel good about your ability to vividly image the everyday scenarios, picture yourself at the driving range. See the range in front of you, the grass underfoot, hear the sound of the ball as it makes contact with your club, smell the leather of your glove. What else do you take in as you image this scene? See yourself hit three or four balls, noting your senses as you do.

Visualize this scenario both internally and externally. After going through your imagery session, list what you noticed.

Sight: _____

Sound: _____

Smell: _____

Touch: _____

Taste: _____

When you have the imagery of the range down, try picturing yourself on the course. Set the scene. Are you are playing for fun with friends, playing eighteen in a charity tournament for work, or competing in a Pro-Am tournament? Are people watching you? What are you wearing? See yourself preparing for your next shot. Feel your confidence and the butterflies in your stomach. What are the course conditions? What time of day is it? Are you warm or cold? Perspiring? How does your body feel? What are you thinking about?

Visualize this scenario both internally and externally. After going through your imagery session, list what you noticed.

Sight: _____

Sound: _____

Smell: _____

Touch: _____

Taste: _____

If it was easy for you to pick out the details from the preceding exercises, you are on the right track to achieving vividness. However, if you had difficulty coming up with specifics, you could use some work on creating images filled with detail. Practice! When you image, look carefully at your surroundings and notice what's in the scene. Take "photographs" in your mind of each scene in your mental movie. Press "play," and let the movie run to a new frame; then press "pause" and examine the details there. As your familiarity with this process increases, you can let the whole movie play through, while noticing every detail along the way. The more vivid your images, the more useful they are to your performance.

Also aim to have your images completely under your mind's control. You should eventually be able to break down each skill into tiny pieces, slow it down, see it from all angles, and speed it up. As you learn, you may need to slow the image down quite a bit to get it to do what you want. That's OK—take it slowly, and as you can control it more, speed it up gradually to real-time speed. This controllability is key to achieving peak performance.

Now image the preceding scenes again, starting with the first and working your way through to the last, most challenging exercise. This time try to visualize the scene at a different speed or in a different direc-

tion. Can you see it in slow motion? Try it in fast-forward. Can you reverse the play? Describe.

_____

_____

_____

_____

If you have difficulty mentally creating a picture, there are two easy tricks to help trigger mental images. The first is to look at a photograph or object related to golf; then close your eyes and try to replicate that exact image in your mind. Open your eyes and see the object; then close your eyes and replicate it. Repeating this process should help you see the image on the inside of your eyelids. The second technique is to watch a video of a tour professional or golf instructor playing golf. These days, you can find hundreds of short clips for free online. Play the video for only a few seconds; then replay it in your mind's eye. This should help you focus on the sights, sounds, and feelings of action imagery.

> magine the ball has little legs, and chop them off.
>
> —HENRY COTTON[9]

Remember as well the importance of keeping images positive. Visualize what you want to happen rather than what you do not want to happen. If you do visualize mistakes, stop the mental tape, rewind, and play it through again until you have performed correctly. Continuing to imagine making errors will only strengthen the muscle memory negatively and result in poor performance. Just think, if you are visualizing yourself hitting a ten-foot putt and you continuously miss left, what do you think you are going to do when you are actually on the green with a ten-foot putt in front of you? Fix the errors as quickly as possible and see yourself making the putt, replacing the negative image with one done correctly.

TAKE IT TO THE COURSE!

The next time you go to the driving range, use imagery to build confidence and strengthen muscle memory. Grab your driver, and pick a specific target you'll aim to hit. As you approach the ball, look closely at the target, mentally noting all the details you can. Now close your eyes and mentally replay the picture of your target in your mind, making the picture as vivid as possible. Then visualize yourself hitting this shot toward that target. First, visualize yourself from an internal perspective, seeing the ball and your grip on the club and feeling the swing from your own viewpoint. Then replay the same shot from an external perspective, watching your setup and swinging from a variety of angles. As you prepare to actually hit the shot, hold on to the positive thought or image in your mind to trigger the feeling of a great swing and to block out any last-minute corrections you may be tempted to analyze. Then let your mind go, and send the ball on its way. Repeat this whole process with every ball you address. This is the start to building visualization into your game.

Which positive images or thoughts did you use? What feelings did they trigger?

_____

_____

_____

_____

Were you able to visualize both from the internal and the external perspectives? If not, try slowing down each image: gradually speed up the images as you gain control over them, until you can play them at full speed. Or try watching actual movies or pictures of shots you want to make from each perspective and then instantly replaying them in your own mind.

SUMMARY

In this chapter, you learned the basic brain science showing how visualization works in golf. Specifically, we discussed:

→ Elite athletes of all sports identify visualization as a key part of their mental conditioning.

→ External visualization (to correct mistakes) and internal visualization (to feel the proper technique)—a combination is most beneficial.

→ The body achieves what the mind believes. Use positive images to replace doubts, worries, fears, and mistakes.

→ Imagination principle: you can build confidence and consistency in your strokes by visualizing, since your mind treats real and imagined shots similarly.

→ Muscle memory theory: your muscles physically respond when you mentally rehearse your shots.
→ Visualization improves your muscle memory and activates right-brain performance. Let visualization take the place of thinking.
→ Work hard to control your images and create full and vivid scenes. Incorporate all of the senses into your mental pictures.
→ Think positively; image yourself calm and confident. Give your body the opportunity to follow a positive mind.

Whether it's a two-foot putt or a 300-yard drive, it's the six inches between your ears that determines if you'll make the shot. The mind is the central control that makes your body perform or falter, hit or miss, drain it or lip out. It's the piece of the puzzle that can change any bad day to a good day. Start by visualizing from both perspectives, replacing negative thoughts with positive pictures. With this foundation, you're ready to move onto the chapters that address *how* to make the most of visualization in your game. Just like using the best equipment, learning to consistently use mental imagery can be your ace in the hole.

2

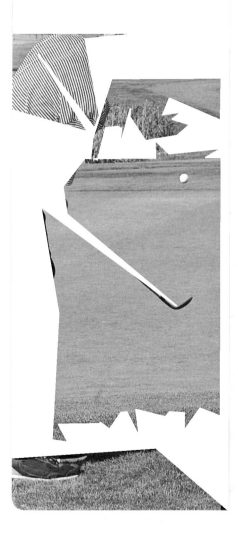

*Visualization
in Action*

Jon is at a point that all athletes find themselves periodically—waiting for something to click and move him up to the next competitive level. Playing with a twelve handicap, Jon has spent the last month on the course tracking his stats carefully. He scores fairways hit, greens hit, number of putts on each hole, and how close he gets bunker and chip shots. After careful calculation, his results show he does a great job hitting the fairways and sinking his putts, but he isn't as strong in getting his chip shots close to the hole.

Determined to figure out what he needs to do to improve his chip shots, he begins to think through a few recent rounds. He attempts to replay several of the holes in his mind, like a movie, seeing each shot from various angles and recalling what he was thinking about before swinging the club each time. As he does this review, Jon realizes that he has tension near the green that makes him nervous. This is normal for many golfers, as hitting a good chip shot can make the difference between putting for birdie or putting for bogey. He also becomes aware that he needs a more fluid motion when chipping. His motion tends to slow down as he comes through the ball, most likely as a result of the tension and nerves he experiences.

Taking from what he already does in his pre-shot routine, Jon decides he will use a few more seconds before every chip shot he attempts and take two or three deep breaths to calm his nerves. He also visualizes himself relaxed and then sees himself make a smooth, clean chip right into playing position on the green. As he watches his swing in his mind, he sees the club moving down and through the ball in a smooth, controlled motion. He then steps up, takes his practice swing, imprints the feel and look of the swing, and immediately addresses the ball. He takes one more deep breath, begins his backswing as he exhales, and swings through the ball.

TEEING OFF

Incorporating visualization into the regular rhythms of your golf game directly impacts the way you play each round. The results are all the evidence you need to believe in the difference made when you see each shot before you swing. We turn from laying the groundwork—that is, providing you with an understanding of how visualization works and why it's important—and move on to giving you actual ways to begin using it in your personal game. Before long, you will find yourself visualizing all the time: in preparing for each shot, seeing the entire hole's layout, and even in readying yourself for a presentation to your boss. Open your mind, and see how you can incorporate this technique into nearly every area of your game.

In this chapter you discover:

→ a plan for integrating visualization into your golf game
→ relaxation techniques to prepare your mind and body for visualization
→ the importance of a pre-shot routine and how to create your own
→ how to create a swing thought and a mantra
→ how to use imagery when you are injured

This is where the real fun begins! Learning how to actually use imagery and incorporate it into your game is where we tee off.

INITIAL TIMETABLE

We set up a tiered system for beginning, intermediate, and advanced visualizers, seen in Tables 2.1, 2.2, and 2.3, respectively. This allows you to get started visualizing and seeing improvements. As you advance through the stages, keep practicing the skills and exercises learned in the prior stage. If you already have some experience imaging, jump in at the stage appropriate for you. To help you decide the right level for you, see your score on the Self-Assessment Scorecard to determine where to begin.

If you have little to no experience visualizing and scored between 66 and 90 on the Self-Assessment Scorecard, or if you just lack confidence in your imaging ability, we encourage you to start at the very beginning and work your way through each of the stages. This takes time and patience, but it is more beneficial to you than trying to jump into a level of visualizing above your capability. If, as you gain confidence, you believe you can skip ahead, feel free to give it a try! Don't be afraid to back up a week or spend two weeks on one level to make sure you have it down.

Self-Assessment Scorecard questions 1, 2, and 21 describe what and where you currently visualize. Considering your overall score and your imagery level, what do you believe is the appropriate level of visualization for you to practice?

Be patient and know that mastering imagery takes practice and time, much like any physical skill. Just like learning a physical skill, the more repetition the better. You may start out frustrated and lose interest because you can't create and control images instantly. Stick with it! As

TABLE 2.1 *Beginning Visualization*

Stage	What to Visualize	Where to Visualize	Frequency and Duration
1	Choose a simple and familiar task such as brushing your teeth or tying your shoes.	Find a comfortable location with minimal distractions. For example, your bedroom, the couch, a backyard chair.	Practice for one week, daily for 5–10 minutes.
2	The same simple and familiar task from Stage 1.	Place yourself in a somewhat distracting environment. For example, while working out, having the television or stereo playing, walking between classes or meetings.	Practice for about two weeks, 3–5 times each week for 5–15 minutes.
3	Visualize yourself at the driving range. Take in the whole scene, and then focus just on yourself and your swing.	Find a comfortable location with minimal distractions.	Practice for one week, daily for 10–15 minutes.
4	Just as in Stage 3, visualize yourself at the driving range.	As in Stage 2, place yourself in a somewhat distracting environment.	Practice for one to two weeks; 3–5 times a week for 10–15 minutes.
5	Your pre-shot routine. Once you have your pre-shot routine down, visualize yourself running through your pre-shot routine and then actually striking the ball.	Find a comfortable location with minimal distractions.	Practice for one week, 3–5 times daily for 10–15 minutes.

your visualization ability progresses and you become very comfortable with it, you will be able to image even when you are high on adrenaline, when you are tense and nervous, and with your eyes open. As you go through the stages, keep your images vivid, within your control, and positive. Practice visualizing both internally and externally. With consistent practice, you can really get good at it.

TABLE 2.2 *Intermediate Visualization*

Stage	What to Visualize	Where to Visualize	Frequency and Duration
6	Visualize yourself playing a hole on your home course from start to finish. Be sure to include your pre-shot routine.	Find a comfortable location with minimal distractions. As visualizing becomes easier, put yourself in more distracting environments.	Practice for one week, 3–5 times daily for 10–15 minutes.
7	Visualize yourself playing a selection of holes on your home course.	Find a comfortable location with minimal distractions. As visualizing becomes easier, put yourself in more distracting environments.	Practice 2–3 times weekly.
8	Use the imagery scripts in Chapter 7. Choose a few that address the parts of your game you are working to improve. Create a recording of the script that you can follow by listening.	Find a comfortable location with minimal distractions. As visualizing becomes easier, put yourself in more distracting environments. If you have a recording, you could visualize in the car or anywhere you can listen to an MP3 player.	Practice 2–3 times weekly or as needed.
9	Design your own script using the instructions in Chapter 8. Create a recording of the script that you can follow by listening.	Find a comfortable location with minimal distractions. As visualizing becomes easier, put yourself in more distracting environments. If you have a recording, you could visualize in the car or anywhere you can listen to an MP3 player.	Practice 2–3 times weekly or as needed.

This skill truly takes time and effort, but there's a bonus to this practice: each time you visualize mentally, you also improve your physical preparation. Thus, you get a double payback on your training. Have faith—visualization is one of the most powerful tools of performance

TABLE 2.3 *Advanced Visualization*

Stage	What to Visualize	Where to Visualize	Frequency and Duration
10	Visualize different scenarios of your toughest shots.	Anywhere possible: in the car, on your couch, on a bike ride, at the mall, etc.	Practice at least 2–3 times weekly and as needed.
11	Changing your swing, grip, address, posture, or whatever else you want to alter. Videotape yourself from all angles. Analyze the video with your instructor or coach and determine what changes need to be made. Before ever swinging a club or addressing the ball, visualize how you want the new swing to look, feel, and sound.	Anywhere possible.	Practice daily for 10–15 minutes.
12	Golf drills. Whether you are learning the correct clubhead path for a chip shot, putting with one hand to emphasize your guiding hand controlling the stroke, or trying to detect an improper weight shift, use visualization to practice these drills both before you first try the drill and in times when you can't get to the course to practice.	Wherever you prefer.	Regularly. Whenever you play and as needed off the course.

enhancement and well worth the effort to perfect. Once you are comfortable with all thirteen stages, share with someone else how to incorporate visualization into his or her golf game. Pass on this skill to others, helping them improve their game too.

Stage	What to visualize	Where to visualize	Frequency & Duration
13	Course management. What better way to work on course management than to practice it first in your mind? Play through a variety of holes, changing the lie of the ball with each mental swing. Determine what club you should hit with next. Strengthen your familiarity with your clubs—in what situations to use them, how they respond, and what works best—by trying them out in your mind. You must first have an understanding of your clubs before attempting this stage.	Wherever you prefer.	Regularly. Whenever you play and as needed off the course.

COACH'S CORNER

For your players to believe visualization can help their game, you have to believe it for yourself. Make sure you are working on using imagery in your own game and advancing through the stages, attempting more challenging types of imagery. Practice visualizing with your players, and give them examples of how you have used it in your game. If you haven't tried it or don't buy it, your players won't either.

On the Self-Assessment Scorecard, question 20 asked where you can image most clearly. Your surroundings when you visualize can often be duplicated or simulated elsewhere. For example, if you image while walking to class or a meeting even with the distractions of others passing by, you may also image well on the driving range, with similar visual and auditory distractions all around. Think about how you can replicate your favorite imagery place in other settings. Write down what you can do to be able to facilitate using imagery on the course.

_____

_____

_____

_____

FIRST THINGS FIRST: RELAXATION

It is important, especially if you are not very experienced with imagery, to take the time to relax prior to an imagery session. Being relaxed helps you focus better. There are many different methods of relaxation. Determine what works best for you, and spend a few moments destressing before you begin visualizing. Ahead are two short relaxation exercises to try. Relaxation is addressed further in Chapter 4 with full versions of these techniques.

Calming Breath Exercise

The calming breath exercise is great to use when you need to calm yourself quickly.[1]

1. Breathing from your abdomen, inhale slowly to a count of five (count slowly "one . . . two . . . three . . . four . . . five" as you inhale).
2. Pause and hold your breath to a count of five.
3. Exhale slowly, through your nose or mouth, to a count of five (or more if it takes you longer). Be sure to exhale fully.
4. When you've exhaled completely, take two breaths in your normal rhythm; then repeat steps 1 through 3 in the preceding cycle.
5. Keep up the exercise for at least five minutes. This should involve going through at least ten cycles of in five, hold five, out five. Remember to take two normal breaths between each cycle. If you start to feel light-headed while practicing this exercise, stop for thirty seconds and then start again.
6. Throughout the exercise, keep your breathing smooth and regular, without gulping in breaths or breathing out suddenly.

Try it!

Use an abbreviated version of this exercise when you are on the course and feeling uptight. Rather than taking five minutes for the exercise, take one minute or even fifteen seconds. Take two to three deep abdominal breaths. Use this regularly to trigger your body into a relaxed physical and mental state.

Progressive Muscle Relaxation Technique

Progressive muscle relaxation (PMR) involves a series of contracting and relaxing exercises targeting all the major muscle groups of the body.[2] Hold each contraction for ten seconds, and sustain relaxation periods for fifteen to twenty seconds, giving you time to become fully aware of how a tense body part feels versus how a relaxed body part feels. Maintain your focus on the targeted muscle group. Each time you contract a muscle group, tighten the specified muscles as hard as you can without hurting yourself, while keeping the rest of the body relaxed. Then release the contraction abruptly and allow full relaxation. If you find a particularly tight muscle group, contract and relax it two or three times before moving on.

The following is a very brief script for the PMR technique to help you understand how the method works.

1. To begin, find a comfortable place to sit or lie down, and close your eyes. Take three deep abdominal breaths, exhaling slowly each time. As you exhale, imagine that tension throughout your body begins to flow away.
2. Clench your fists. Hold for ten seconds, and then release for fifteen to twenty seconds. Use the same time intervals for all other muscle groups.
3. Tighten your biceps by drawing your forearms up toward your shoulder and "making a muscle" with both arms. Hold . . . and then relax.
4. Tighten your triceps—the muscles on the undersides of your upper arms—by extending your arms out straight and locking your elbows. Hold . . . and then relax.
5. Tense the muscles in your forehead by raising your eyebrows as far as you can. Hold . . . and then relax. Imagine your forehead muscles becoming smooth and limp as they relax.

Go on to contracting and relaxing the face, jaw, neck, shoulders, upper back, chest, stomach, lower back, buttocks, thighs, calves, feet, and toes, as further described in Chapter 4. Always try to finish with a few final deep breaths.

Try it!

This exercise, too, can be shortened for the course. Once you are comfortable with PMR, you can scan your body for areas of tension and then focus on relaxing those specific muscle groups. Often you'll find that your shoulders and neck bear the bulk of the load. Rather than contracting and relaxing each muscle group, hone in on the one or two areas of greatest tightness. Tense the muscles in that area for ten seconds, and then release for the regular fifteen to twenty seconds. You can quickly and effectively release tension from that muscle group with a few contract-relax cycles.

APPLY THAT IMAGERY!

Now that you have all this information about imagery, we want you to learn a few methods for using it on the course. The following questions and exercise help you hone your personal pre-shot patterns and routines, leading to consistently successful performances.

Pre-Shot Routines

One of the best things you can do for your game is to incorporate a pre-shot routine. Moments of "flow" tend to come when your body is relaxed, your critical mind is turned off, your creative mind is engaged, and your muscles can react the way they have been trained. The pre-shot routine establishes something familiar that you do every single time you address the ball. This familiarity releases your left brain from the over-thinking that leads to the "analysis paralysis" syndrome and gives your right brain the freedom to create an image of your next shot.

Your routine may include elements such as lining up behind the ball, focusing in on your target, imaging how the swing will feel, taking deep breaths, adjusting your glove, hearing the sound of your clubface making contact with the ball, tapping the end of the club on the ground, taking two practice swings, waggling your clubhead, repeating your swing thought, or any number of other habits. Trevor Immelman, 2008 Masters Champion, has a distinct pre-shot routine. He stands behind the ball

> t doesn't matter what your pre-shot routine is, just as long as you do it the same way every time . . .
>
> —*TIGER WOODS*[3]

and points the club shaft over the ball to his target. He says it helps him get a visual image of the shot he's about to play. When he's satisfied with the image, he walks a half circle to the ball and then prepares the set-up position. Always the same motions, in the same order, every time. It doesn't matter if he's hitting off the practice tee or in a major championship: he does this on every single full shot.[4] This pre-shot routine helps him focus; by concentrating on his familiar ritual, he can feel comfortable, less nervous, and more prepared.

Build imagery into your pre-shot routine to strengthen the mind-body connection and to help remind the muscles how you want them to respond. If your pre-shot routine begins as you stand behind the ball looking at your target, perhaps that's where you take an extra second to visualize your perfect swing. Hank Haney, swing coach to Tiger Woods, says, "Watch a tour player go through his pre-shot routine, and you'll almost never see him walk in from the side and make a practice swing right next to the ball. He faces the target from behind the ball, to visualize his shot, and makes a couple of gentle practice swings with his eyes on the target before stepping in."[5] However, if your routine begins at address, see that incredible swing in the moments as you settle into your position. Even in these brief imagery moments, remember to make your images vivid, controllable, and positive. If you find yourself doubting or questioning, take a step back and start your routine again.

An additional mental component to consider including in your pre-shot routine is deciding to accept the results. Whether they are good or bad, accepting the results before they happen releases you from the pressure of the present shot. Now don't get too far ahead of yourself and begin thinking about your next shot. Remain in the present, but be willing to accept the shot no matter what the lie. By learning to accept the result regardless of what it is, you can limit the negative self-talk that comes after a poorly hit shot and the self-doubt that you may face before even starting your backswing. You are free to focus on your pre-shot routine and then simply on your shot.[6]

To get the most out of your pre-shot routine, incorporate it every single time you prepare to make a shot. Then no matter what the situation, your pre-shot routine is a regular part of your performance. Whether you are on the driving range, the putting green, or the sixteenth hole, use it. If you are a competitive golfer, using your pre-shot routine helps make competition feel more like practice, which may help you overcome nerves and distractions. If you play just for fun and exercise, it helps bring greater consistency to your game.

Self-Assessment Scorecard question 8 refers to your use of a pre-shot routine. Take this time to create the best pre-shot routine for you. What would you like to do before each shot? Keep it simple. If you currently use a pre-shot routine, is there anything you would like to modify? Watch the PGA Tour players' routines. Are there parts of their routines that you want to emulate? You may even write down a few routine options that you want to try the next time you're out on the course. Try them out first on the driving range, get the routine down, and then take it to the course.

COMMIT TO YOUR SHOT

Matt

The biggest reason I believe players miss shots is a failure to commit. That is why my pre-shot preparation is so important. I start this process around twenty yards behind the ball as I walk up to it. I'm looking for the conditions of the ball—whether it's in the fairway or the rough, how far away I am from the green, and what type of trouble is ahead. This doesn't take long, and by the time I reach the ball, I'm now searching my target. Once I figure where I'm going, I challenge myself to make sure this is the correct shot and confirm that I'm not trying to exceed my limits. Then I select the appropriate club. From there I take a practice swing, then move behind the ball, and image the ball in flight to my target. I set up the club to my target and settle in checking my stance and alignment. Then one more time, I visualize hitting the ball just as I had done a few seconds prior and hit the shot. The preparations I have gone through instill confidence and a commitment to execute the shot. As a collegiate golf coach, I encourage my players to do the same mental preparation.

Swing Thought

One way to help trigger positive images is through cue words or actions in the form of a swing thought. Swing thoughts are typically used to give yourself an instructional reminder about what you want your body to do as you swing the club. You may associate certain words or actions with certain feelings that direct your mind and energy to what you want your body to do. For example, before you swing, you may think "soft hands" to keep your hands relaxed when you hold the club, "smooth tempo" to remind yourself to pace your swing, or "commit" to make sure you leave it all on the course. Butch Harmon, swing coach to Phil Mickelson, suggests using "swing to a finish" as a reminder to right-handers to finish with your weight shifted to your left side and your body positioned over your left leg.[7] Fred Funk uses the word *connected* to remember that his shoulders, arms and hands, and the club extending out should create a triangle when he lines up a shot.[8] Fred Couples, on the other hand, says he likes to keep things as simple as possible. His swing thought is "Take the club back and hit it."[9]

Creating an image to associate with your swing thought gives you not just a word describing what you wish to do, but also a picture of that desired action. This is all part of shutting down the critical thinking, left side of the brain and opening up the creative right side of the brain where images come from and out of which peak performances flow. Keeping with the previous examples, when you say "soft hands" to yourself, picture yourself holding a small bird or a piece of fine glass. As you think "smooth tempo," picture the pendulum of a grandfather clock keeping perfect pace or even picture yourself as the clock and your club as the pendulum keeping time. When you want to remind yourself to "commit," try picturing yourself completely satisfied knowing you gave the game all your mental and physical energy.

You do want to be careful to do your thinking before you actually swing. Activating these cues as you make your practice swing helps the brain stop thinking and start doing. As you take your practice swings and repeat your swing thoughts, lock in this swing. Once you are locked in, address the ball and simply repeat the swing you just practiced. Your body and mind learn to coordinate in response to these cues because you practice them often in your mind and in physical practice. When the big shot comes, your mind and body will be aligned, and the quick reminders will set you up.

Create and write two to four swing thoughts to help you focus on the positives and what you want to accomplish. These cues may be verbal or physical. The important thing is that they trigger confident images in your mind. Try using these swing thoughts the next time you play.

	CUE	IMAGE THAT IT TRIGGERS
1.	_____	_____
	_____	_____
2.	_____	_____
	_____	_____
3.	_____	_____
	_____	_____
4.	_____	_____
	_____	_____

My Mental Mantra

It also may be helpful for you to create a "mental mantra." A mantra is something you can repeat and focus on to help you block out the overanalytical negative thinking and distractions that can get in the way of a great swing. Should negative thoughts or distractions arise, you can block them out by concentrating on and repeating your mental mantra. We encourage you to choose a positive statement that triggers relevant images. Make it catchy so you remember it well. It may be as simple as a phrase that creates images of you achieving the goal before you, such as "I can do it!" or "I believe." Or it may give you an image of an attitude you want to convey like "Strong and sure," to display confidence or "In the driver's seat," to articulate being in control.

A mental mantra differs from a swing thought in that it can be used in *any* situation, not exclusively before you swing. Consider it almost like a security blanket: you can rely on it under all circumstances to be there to calm, comfort, and focus you. Just like having your childhood teddy bear or blanket, having a mental mantra in your head allows you to relax and block out distracting negative thoughts. You can keep your mental mantra with you always and go to it consistently.

Come up with a mental mantra specific to your aspirations and your style. You may want to pick a few important skills or techniques or goals, or you may

> When I think about three things during my swing, I'm playing poorly; when I think about two things, I have a chance to shoot par; when I think of only one thing, I could win the tournament.
>
> —BOBBY JONES[10]

find that attitudes are more pertinent for you. Take your time, as this is something very personal to you. Be creative and have fun!

Use this mental mantra every time you're on the course or range. You can use it to motivate and energize yourself, to refocus, and to boost your confidence. You can use it to trigger positive images when you're nervous, to psych yourself up before an important tournament or round, and to keep calm under pressure.

IMAGERY WHEN INJURED

Whether or not you have suffered from one yet, at some point in your golf career you will most likely experience injury. Approximately three to five million athletes are injured every year. For golfers, injury could mean back pain, tendonitis, a torn rotator cuff, a sprained ankle, or something more severe. Being injured is not usually enjoyable, but the good news is, using visualization as well as other mental training methods in cooperation with a physical rehabilitation regimen has been proven to reduce the time it takes to heal and to get back to play. Imagery is fairly simple to integrate into your rehab program. Just add up all the time you will spend with an ice or heat pack on your injured body part and utilize that time to practice imagery. Being diligent in visualizing while injured not only helps your body heal more quickly, it helps you mentally prepare to return to the course and it keeps your skills sharp. Here are four specific ways you can implement visualization when you are injured.

Visualize Healing

The principle of dominant thought states that whatever dominates your thoughts is what your body moves toward. If your mind is focused on your body healing, you will help promote the recovery process. You might visualize your broken bone being fused back together or the cells of your torn ligament joining together to build a stronger ligament. Some may even picture small, imaginary characters working inside your body to build it back up. Some of this may sound a bit silly, but it really has been proven to work!

Visualize Practice

One of the most difficult aspects of injury is missing time from playing the game you love. Skills can become rusty if you are out of practice for a few weeks or months. There is no substitute for practice, but the next best thing is using imagery to work on skills that you cannot physically practice. This helps you come back to the game at a level close to where you left when you became injured. You could picture yourself hitting through a bucket of balls or replay some of your best shots or holes played. Play through an imaginary game at your favorite course. You might even try working on a skill that you had not quite mastered prior to injury or setting your mind on learning a new skill. Perhaps you have wanted to refine your flop shot or maybe work on a controlled draw. Why not give it a try in your mind first, and then take it to the course when you're healthy? The time spent in rehab won't set you back as far if you're continuously imaging your skills.

> ### PLAYER'S POINTER
>
> Especially while injured, visualization can be a valuable substitute for physical workouts. Of course, it can't replace physical practice, but it can still help you maintain your skill level when injured. Rather than becoming frustrated, you can rehearse skills in your mind, perfect your techniques, and strengthen your muscle memory by becoming more aware of how your skills should feel. When you return to the course, you will be well prepared to perform, because you have been repeating your drives, chips, and putts in your mind. Like pro players who repeatedly use imagery to speed recovery, you, too, can picture your body healing and returning to peak form.

Visualize Coping

Do you have any fears about returning to play? It's very common to be afraid of being reinjured or doing the same thing that led to your original injury. Or perhaps you are recovering from an injury you have faced time and time again; you are tired of being injured, but don't know how to avoid it. Visualize yourself coming up against the obstacles you fear and then overcoming those barriers successfully. This can also be helpful if you have fears during the injury recovery process. Maybe there is a particular exercise that is difficult for you or you are nervous about walking without your crutches or running again for the first time. It could even be something outside of the specific rehab process, like hearing your doctor say you cannot compete for an extended period of time. By first overcoming whatever conjures up fear and anxiety inside, you can deal with it mentally before you return to play.

Visualize Success

How do you feel when the other golfers in your group congratulate you for a great shot? What about your feelings when you have a great round of golf and nail every key shot? How about the simple times when you are at the driving range by yourself and hit a sweet shot? Visualizing yourself being successful on the course or the range helps bring these motivating and energizing feelings back into your mind to build your confidence and just make you feel good. Re-creating scenes that actually took place in the past or creating new scenes depicting what you want to see happen when you come back to participate are great places to start.

Which method(s) of imagery are you most likely to use when you are injured? How do you see yourself using that particular style? Try practicing at least one of the imagery techniques now. If you are currently injured, create a plan for including imagery in your daily rehab routine.

_____

_____

_____

_____

TAKE IT TO THE COURSE!

Try this game the next time you are hitting a bucket of balls at the driving range.

Think of a hole on your home course. Visualize the hole—the distance to the pin, where the hazards are, what the fairway looks like, where the out-of-bounds (OB) markers stand, and anything else you can see. Tee up as if you were actually playing this hole. Look out at the driving range, and replace what you see with your image of this hole. Choose your target. Go through your pre-shot routine like you normally would. Address the ball, bring your club back, and swing through the ball. Did you come close to your target? Did you hit out of bounds? Picture the lie of your ball. If you are out of bounds, hit the next ball as if you were actually out of bounds. If you are lined up perfectly, set up your next shot as such. How far are you from your next target? What club would you use to make the next shot? Put your driver down and pull out the appropriate club. Again, go through your pre-shot routine, position yourself in front of the ball and take your next shot. Where does the ball lie in relation to your intended target? Are you in the greenside bunker?

Did you land on the green? Now when you go to the practice green, try to remember this lie and play out the hole.

You could play an entire eighteen holes using this game. It helps get you in the habit of using your pre-shot routine, encourages you to practice visualizing your target, and can even help you learn better course management.

SUMMARY

This chapter was full of ways to begin refining your visualization practice. Let's recap what we have covered:

→ Be patient with yourself as you begin to work imagery into your golf game. There is a steep learning curve, and it will take time.
→ Relax your body and mind before you spend time visualizing. Create abbreviated relaxation methods you can take to the course.
→ Determine how you will incorporate visualization into your game, and start using it immediately.
→ Remember to use visualization when you are injured and are not out on the course. Incorporating one of the injury imagery methods helps speed your recovery.
→ Give yourself time to get things down. Don't expect perfection immediately. Practice, practice, practice!

With any physical skill, the more you practice, the more easy it becomes. The same is true for visualization. So step out in faith and try it! The more you visualize well, the more your golf performance improves. The integration of the mind and the body in this way helps you move past mediocre play and take your game to the next level. Visualize on the train on your way to work, while walking down the street, lying in bed, and so on. With time and practice, you will create excellent images that make your performance easier and more consistent. Be patient and positive!

HOW FAR HAVE YOU COME?

The questions in this section are designed to assess how far you have come in applying visualization and what you can work on to improve your ability to visualize. Wait until you have had a chance to work through the questions in Chapter 2 and to apply the methods and exercises before completing this section.

1. Do you use both internal and external imagery now? Have you noticed which is more effective for certain tasks?

_____

_____

_____

_____

_____

_____

2. How often do you visualize? Where do you visualize most clearly?

_____

_____

_____

_____

_____

_____

3. How have you incorporated visualization into your golf game? How well do you apply visualization when you're on the driving range or playing a round?

_____

_____

_____

_____

_____

_____

4. How has using visualization enhanced your golf game? What improvements or changes do you notice?

_____

_____

_____

_____

_____

_____

5. What are you still trying to improve in your imagery ability?

_____

_____

_____

_____

_____

_____

6. Reward yourself for getting this far! Take the time to pat yourself on the back and to recognize your efforts in enhancing your mental toughness. Congratulations!

3

Power of the
Positive Mind

L ibby picked up golf about ten years ago as a hobby she could enjoy with her husband. It has also been a great way to be connected at work and in her community by participating in charity tournaments and fun scrambles. She considers herself an average golfer and can keep up with just about any group in which she plays. The more Libby golfs, the more she enjoys the sport.

In the past year, she has become more aware of the mental side of the game and how hard it is for her to recover after a few bad shots in a row. When she has a bad shot, she gets frustrated and is quick to criticize herself. After a couple of poorly played balls, her confidence is so damaged that the rest of the round is hard to recover. She is her own worst enemy when it comes to golf.

She noticed that one of her friends is rarely fazed by a drive out of bounds or a missed putt. Her confidence is obvious, but Libby just isn't sure how to get there. Curious to know her secret, Libby asked her about it the last time they played together. "Well, it's not always easy," said the friend. "It has taken a lot of work, but what I've learned is that I have to remember to think positively and stick to my routine. If I make a bad shot, I try to quickly replace the negative feelings with positive ones, by reminding myself that my game is not defined by that shot and by imagining how I want the next shot to feel. I can't give myself the option of thinking about the mistake I just made. What's done is done: I can only control what's next."

It sounded somewhat simple, so Libby began to try out her friend's suggestions. At first it was hard. She was accustomed to reacting in a certain way to poorly played balls and bad decisions. She had to rewire her brain to think positively. Over the next several months, she began to notice improvements in play and an increase in her confidence. At the present time, Libby is still working on developing a more positive mind. She hasn't eliminated negative thinking entirely, but she is learning to deal more effectively with the thoughts she does have. She has found that she enjoys the game even more. And after a day on the course, she can walk off more confident in her game and excited about the next opportunity to play.

TEEING OFF

Self-confidence is an essential element of consistent success in golf as well as in any other performance in life.[1] Golfers and sport psychologists alike agree that confidence is a distinguishing characteristic that separates the very successful from the lackluster athletes.[2] Confidence affects every aspect of your golf game. Without it, success is difficult to achieve. Visualizing yourself having confidence is an important step toward believing you have the ability to reach your golfing potential.

The goals of this chapter are to:

→ assess your own confidence
→ demonstrate the power of positive thinking and how it can boost confidence
→ describe how your thoughts dictate your actions
→ teach you how to develop a consistently positive mind-set

BECOMING A CONFIDENT GOLFER

Self-confidence is defined simply as a belief in your ability to "get things done." In golf this translates into the belief you have in your ability to succeed on the course.[3] If you are a confident golfer, you feel optimistic about your ability to perform and feel in control of that ability.[4] It is important to remember that your ability does not decrease—even if you are injured or if you are in a slump and haven't made a good shot in quite a while. If you have done it once, you have the ability to do it again.[5] If you go out and play the best round of your life, it is because you have the ability to do so and that capacity is not going to change. That does not necessarily mean you *will* do it again, but you have the *ability* to do so.

Your personal confidence level is based on your perception of your ability. In other words, for your confidence to be stable, it must be based on an accurate awareness of your current level of ability. If you believe you are able to drive the ball 350 yards on this shot, but the farthest you have ever hit the ball is 250 yards, your perception of your ability is inaccurate. Perhaps with time and practice you will be able to drive the ball 300 yards or maybe even a bit farther, but self-confidence is based on the present reality and attainable future goals. Believing you have the ability to hit the ball 300 yards is more reasonable, considering that others of a similar skill level as you have achieved that distance. Alternatively, if you have a consistent fade shot, but happen to shank a few, you should still have confidence in your fade, because you trust your ability based upon your previous experience. Correct assessment of your ability helps you create an accurate perception and thereby an unswerving self-confidence.

See Self-Assessment Scorecard question 10 for your current level of golf confidence. What specific skills do you perform with confidence, and in which areas do you lack confidence?

_____

_____

_____

_____

_____

In what circumstances has your perception of your ability as a golfer changed for the better or for the worse?

_____

_____

_____

_____

_____

Because perceptions are always changing, there is no guarantee you will be confident 100 percent of the time. Fortunately, the techniques described in this chapter help you play more confidently in more rounds of golf. Often, perceptions change when you underperform and subsequently let the resulting negative thoughts influence your belief in your ability. Consistently practicing positive imagery, rooting yourself in reality while also remembering what you are capable of achieving, is important to keeping perceptions from changing as a result of one bad shot or one bad round. Perceptions may also change if you make an extraordinary play. Because you have done it once, you can certainly do it again, but make sure to set reasonable expectations of yourself. Consider the things you did correctly on that amazing shot, imprint them in your brain, and then factor those into an imagery sequence with the goal of replicating both the feeling of elation as well as the technique, pre-shot routine, positive thinking, and anything else that made it possible.

In your mind, replay a time when you hit an extraordinary shot. List the elements that made this shot possible; then create a short imagery sequence highlighting what you did well.

_____

_____

_____

_____

_____

_____

How have you noticed your confidence change within a round of golf or a tournament?

_____

_____

_____

_____

When you feel you are confident of a skill, what makes you feel that way?

_____

_____

_____

_____

When you experience mental blocks and fears, or the yips, what triggers them?

_____

_____

_____

_____

Confidence and Performance

Confidence and performance are directly related.[6] As your performance improves, confidence grows. As performance declines, confidence drops. The opposite is true as well: as confidence increases, performance gets better; as confidence declines, performance suffers. It's an easy concept to grasp and to relate to your own experiences.

Think of confidence on a continuum that ranges from low confidence, when you do not believe you have the ability to be successful, to overconfidence, a misperceived confidence resulting from an inaccurate belief in your ability. At any given point during play, you are somewhere along this continuum. Ideally, you want to be somewhere in the middle of these two extremes.[7]

Although it might seem you'd rather be overconfident than underconfident, both have their own risks. If you lack confidence in an area of your golf game, you believe you are unlikely to achieve. This lack of confidence usually occurs when you are in pressured situations or after you make mistakes (which may lead to more pressure or mistakes). If you do not believe you have what it takes to get the job done and begin to expect that you will fail, it is likely failure will be the outcome.[8] If you hit into the water hazard on the last hole and the upcoming hole also has a water hazard, your confidence in your ability to hit the fairway and avoid the hazard may be quite low.

On the flip side, if you are overconfident, your inaccurate perception of your ability may also result in a poor play. Overconfidence can lead to a lack of preparation. You may decide you don't need that last practice session at the driving range or you don't need to visualize the more challenging holes on the course. This lack of physical and mental preparation may result in a higher score than you are capable of shooting. Also, if you are overconfident, you may be more likely to try out shots and techniques you wouldn't normally attempt and probably don't have the skill to make. Consider some of the incredible shots you have seen the pros make. Unless you are playing on the Pro Tour or have the skill and technique to be at that level, leave those shots to them and set your sights on what is truly within your grasp.[9, 10]

COACH'S CORNER

Take note of your players' performances, and try to recognize when they are at their optimal confidence level. If players lack confidence, make a point to offer positive encouragement and to give a technical drill whose focus will help them gain confidence. For players who are overconfident, help them by assigning them a challenging task.

Found living somewhere in the middle of overconfidence and underconfidence is ideal confidence. This optimal confidence leads to the best performances on the course. If you have an optimal level of self-confidence, you have a realistic belief in your ability to play great golf. You know you can get the job done, and you do what it takes. You know what you are capable of, you take the time to visualize yourself achieving your goals, and you work hard to reach them. Having this perfect confidence does not exempt you from making mistakes, but it does make you more likely to deal with them positively, learning from them and making improvements for next time.[11, 12]

Name specific situations in which you tend to lack confidence, be overconfident, and have optimal confidence.

Lack of confidence:

_____

Overconfidence:

_____

Optimal confidence:

_____

Keep reading to learn how to boost and maintain your confidence.

THINKING, FEELING, AND PERFORMING

Confidence can instill within you a fire that keeps you moving in a direction toward better and better performances. Remember in the first chapter where it says the body achieves what the mind believes? The idea that your body responds to your mind is clearly displayed when you look at how positive or negative thoughts impact feelings of confidence and thereby performance. Thoughts such as "I can" or "I will" translate into positive feelings of confidence that produce positive behaviors like a smooth and steady swing moving perfectly inside out, which in turn helps you achieve a lower score on the course. However, negative thoughts such as "I can't" or "I'm not good enough" create feelings of self-doubt and a lack of self-confidence. When you find yourself thinking in this manner, you are more likely to end up in the rough or the water.

The expectations of others can also manipulate your thinking and ultimately affect the outcome of play. Your coach wants you to do this and your parents want you to do that, and your teammates and other competitors expect a certain type of play from you. The idea of expectations predicting performance is described by the self-fulfilling prophecy.[13] Simply put, the self-fulfilling prophecy claims that what you believe about yourself and what you think others believe about you have the potential to influence your behavior. Not all golfers fall into this expectation hazard, but it can be challenging to avoid. The good news is it is completely within your control. You decide how expectations will influence your game.

You can choose to begin a cycle of either positive thinking, positive feeling, and positive play, or negative thinking, negative feeling, and negative play. Positive play produces more positive thoughts, leading to greater feelings of confidence and more successful play at each hole, and the cycle continues. This is also true of poor performance, which leads to more negative thoughts, a decrease in confidence, an increase in missed shots and poorly played balls, and inadequate course management, which creates more destructive thoughts, and so on. This devastating snowball effect can run right over you. All the more reason to read on and discover how to rout those negatives and develop a positive mind-set.

> To sink the ball in the hole, you must think the ball in the hole.
>
> —BOB ROSBURG[14]

FIGURE 3.1 *The cycle of influence. Thoughts influence feelings, which influence behavior, and so on.*

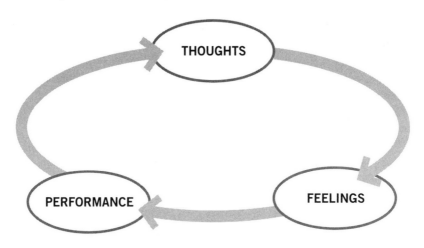

See Self-Assessment Scorecard question 9 to see how you view your ability to be in control of your thoughts and feelings.

The Key Is Consistency

Controlling your thoughts so that they are consistently positive is the key to being consistently confident.[15, 16] If you are confident, then you aren't worried about trying to figure out how to avoid a hazard or what you need to do to stay out of the rough. Rather, your focus is on what it takes to be successful on the next shot. You visualize yourself being confident at the tee, fairway, green, and even in the sand or the rough.[17]

If you are confident, you are more likely to think positively and set goals that challenge you to play your best. You are also more likely to put in the time and energy that is needed to attain your goals. As these goals are achieved, confidence increases and you are more likely to put forth the effort needed to reach your new goal.[18] Your positive thoughts allow you to focus on what you have to do to be successful and motivate you to work hard to achieve your goals. When your goals are met and confidence improves, more positive thoughts are produced, furthering the cycle.

MIND GAMES

Michael

Soft hands. Center cut. Gut this putt. You the man! These are the thoughts and phrases constantly swirling around in my mind during tournament play to keep me playing loose and having fun. The power of positive thinking has consistently helped me beat players who have more talent and practice more often than I do. Conversely, I've noticed over the years that when I start playing poorly, it is because the opposite, negative thoughts creep into my head: *Tense hands. Don't snap hook it. Don't three-putt. You hack.*

I am an emotional golfer. Funneling this energy into positive thinking has led to results that far exceeded my expectations. During my sophomore year of college, nobody gave our golf team a chance to qualify for Nationals. We had to beat a team who had won twelve of the previous thirteen conference championships and thoroughly dominated us the entire season. Playing two man for our team, I found myself in second place overall after the first day. The next day I was paired with the top three golfers in the conference and was under tremendous pressure to help my team knock off the undisputed favorites. What happened? I matched my first day score, finished second overall, and led our team to a shocking upset that landed us in the National Championship at Southern Hills Country Club. On the most pressure-filled stage, I was able to deliver because of the positive thoughts circulating in my mind.

Recall a time when your exceptional play on one hole carried over to the next. What were your thoughts as you prepared yourself for the next shot? What did you visualize?

_____

_____

_____

Describe a time when your negative thoughts and beliefs resulted in a disappointing performance. What negative images and thoughts did you have? How did you react the next time you had to perform?

COACH'S CORNER

You may be thinking, "What else can I do to help my players improve their confidence?" Here are some tips:[19]

→ Use peer modeling instead of expert modeling.

→ Pair confident and unconfident athletes at the same skill level together for drills in practice.

→ Do not give your players false confidence by telling them they can do something when you don't believe they can. If the players fail after you have convinced them that they will succeed, their confidence may sink even lower.

→ Help your players focus on the technical aspects of their performances rather than the final outcome.

→ Use more short-term goals—the more small improvements your athletes see, the more their self-confidence will rise.

Developing a Positive Mind

As we stated before, the key to optimal self-confidence is consistent positive thinking. The key to consistent positive thinking is learning how to control your thinking. If you can learn how to control your thinking, you will be well on your way to a more consistent golf game. Every time you have a thought, whether it is actually verbalized or just stays in your head, it can be considered that you are, in essence, talking to yourself. This self-talk is the constant, ongoing conversation that takes place in your mind.[20] The conversation in your head runs at about 1,000 words per minute. Quite a conversation—during a four-hour round of golf, that's a whopping 240,000 words!

Essentially, self-talk is either positive or negative. You have already read about the impact that positive and negative self-talk (thoughts) have on your feelings and behaviors and have seen that positive thoughts promote success, and improved confidence and negative thoughts promote poor play and lowered confidence. Therefore, it makes sense that we want to figure out how to get rid of the negative and promote the positive. However, learning to think effectively takes time and a lot of practice.[21, 22] But this is the way, and it all begins in your mind!

The first step to taking control of your thinking is to figure out what it is that you are actually thinking. Not only do you need to know what you are saying, you need to know when you speak to yourself, how often and in what situations you tend to talk, and you need to be specific. By doing this, you should be able to determine the precise things you say to yourself before, during, and after you have good and bad performances.[23]

Refer to Self-Assessment Scorecard question 11 to remember how effective you are at stopping negative self-talk.

Over the next few weeks of practice and play, keep a specific written log of your thoughts, noting at what point in the game they occurred, what events led to the thoughts, and how the thoughts impacted your play. If doing this during a round of golf seems too cumbersome or you aren't planning to play a round for a while, try replaying a round, or at least a few holes, in your own mental imagery movie. After you are done, count how many of your thoughts were negative and how many were positive.

SPECIFIC THOUGHT	WHAT CIRCUMSTANCES LED TO THAT THOUGHT?	RESULT

Another simple way to see exactly how many negative thoughts you are having during a round is the positive paper clip exercise.[24] Place a handful of paper clips in the right pocket of your pants when you head out to the course. As you play a round, any time a negative thought arises, take one paper clip and move it to the left pocket. At the end of the round, count how many paper clips, or negative thoughts, you have collected. See the rest of the positive paper clip exercise later in this chapter to learn how to change your negative mind-set to a positive one.

Having this information allows you to stop your negative thoughts before they start. If you know that when you address the ball you start having self-defeating thoughts such as, "I'm definitely not going to hit this fairway," or "Don't top the ball," you need to be able to turn your thinking around before you even step near the tee box. Once you recognize the situations that lead to negative thoughts, as well as the specific negative thoughts that you have, you can then determine a method for controlling self-talk that best suits you.

The next step toward having a positive mind-set is learning how to get rid of your negative thoughts. Several techniques have been developed to teach thought control. Keep in mind that none of these thought-control methods will work unless you know what your negative thoughts are and in what circumstances they happen. Once you have successfully completed the previous exercises, you can begin to try out different thought-controlling techniques. It is important that you find one (or a combination of two or more) that works for you and begin to use it regularly. Thought control is a *skill*, and as with any skill, time and practice are needed to become highly effective. Don't be discouraged if the method you choose doesn't work right away. Keep practicing!

> **f there is doubt in your mind over a golf shot, how can your muscles know what they are expected to do?**
>
> *—HARVEY PENICK*[25]

Picture Perfect. As you know from all you have read so far, the way you think significantly influences your physical actions. When a negative thought comes about, don't just try your hardest to ignore it; actively create an image that gives you a picture of what you want to do instead. Using the previous example, rather than saying, "What if I top the ball?" cover up that thought with a mental picture of what you *do* want to do. Lay the new picture right over the top of the thought so your mind can't even go there. See yourself hitting the ball squarely. You want to see it, feel it, and hear it as well. Then take your stance, and let your body take over.

Looking back at your list of negative thoughts, choose a few you have frequently. Mentally create picture-perfect images you can take to the course and use to shut out the destructive thoughts.

Thought Stopping. This technique uses a cue word or action to stop the negative thought and reminds you to refocus. You can use a trigger such as the word *stop* or *no*, or an action such as snapping a rubber band around your wrist or clapping your hands together. Whatever cue you use, make sure it is something that works for you.[26, 27]

Start by using thought stopping on the driving range or practice green. Use your cue immediately after you have a negative thought or even in the midst of having the thought. As you become comfortable with using this trigger during practice, try using it in a round of golf or even in a tournament.

What cue word or action are you going to use? In what specific situations do you see yourself using this technique?

_____

_____

_____

_____

Thought Changing. As much as we want to do away with negative thoughts completely, the truth of the matter is, they happen.[28] Even tour players have negative thoughts and struggle to take control of their minds. Another method of thought control involves taking the negative thoughts that you have and counteracting them with positive thoughts. By doing this, you are able to give yourself encouragement, refocus your attention on the present situation, and remind yourself that you are in control of your thoughts.

To begin using this technique, it is again important to know what your specific negative thoughts are, in what circumstances they are created, and how they influence your play. For every negative thought you have, a positive replacement statement should be created. Use these statements immediately following a negative thought or string of negative thoughts.

Make a list of the negative thoughts that you typically have and would like to change. Next to each thought, design a positive statement that you can use to replace the negative one. Use the following chart:

NEGATIVE THOUGHT	**POSITIVE REPLACEMENT**
1. _____	_____
_____	_____
2. _____	_____
_____	_____
3. _____	_____
_____	_____
4. _____	_____
_____	_____
5. _____	_____
_____	_____
6. _____	_____
_____	_____
7. _____	_____
_____	_____
8. _____	_____
_____	_____
9. _____	_____
_____	_____
10. _____	_____
_____	_____

Just repeating one positive cue word or phrase replaces negative thoughts and can convince your mind to allow your body to perform at a higher level. Sometimes, the easiest way to boost confidence by replacing negative thoughts is simply to repeat your mental mantra. Remember, the body achieves what the mind believes.

Create two lists. The first list is your self-esteem list. This list should be made up of what you believe are your strengths, positive characteristics, and talents in regard to golf. The second list is your success list.

This list includes all of the successes you have had so far in golf. Nothing is too small. Be completely honest—no one else is going to see these!

SELF-ESTEEM LIST   **SUCCESS LIST**

_____   _____

_____   _____

_____   _____

_____   _____

_____   _____

_____   _____

_____   _____

_____   _____

    Now, keeping in mind what you just wrote, create a third list of specific, action-oriented, positive affirmation statements. Remember to phrase these statements as if you already are what you want to be.

_____

_____

_____

_____

_____

_____

_____

    Once your affirmation statements have been created, use them! Work on one affirmation statement each day. Incorporate your favorite affirmation statement into your imagery scripts and pre-shot routine. Write it down and carry it in your pocket or put it where you will see it frequently. Continuously remind yourself of the statement throughout the day. Repeat it, believe it, and watch it happen!

PLAYER'S POINTER

The warm-up at the start of each practice is a great time to look over your personal list of positive thoughts and affirmations. Keep affirmation reminders in your golf bag. Pull out and review your affirmations at least once before a practice and after a practice to seal the statement in your mind and to promote a positive mind-set.

Positive Paper Clips. This simple, tactile exercise helps you physically remember to replace the negative thoughts you have with positive substitutes, by using paper clips.

As described earlier in this chapter, start by placing a handful of paper clips in the right pocket of your pants when you head out to the course. As you play a round, any time a negative thought arises, take one paper clip and move it to the left pocket. At the end of the round, count how many paper clips, or negative thoughts, you have collected. Do this several times, seeing how many negative thoughts per round you average.[29]

Once you have a feel for the frequency with which you have negative thoughts, try this next step: when you have a negative thought, rather than immediately moving the paper clip to your opposite pocket, substitute the negative thought with a positive image. If you successfully replace the thought, the paper clip remains in the right pocket. If you are not able to control a negative thought with a positive replacement, move a paper clip from the right to the left pocket. Continue to work on reducing the number of uncontrolled negative thoughts each time you play.

If negative thoughts are a significant challenge for you, consider setting a goal to reduce your number of uncontrolled negative thoughts. Reward yourself as steps are made toward achieving this goal, understanding that a positive mind will make the difference in your golf game.

Fudge! Fix, Forget, Focus. This catchy alliteration is a great way to work through a frustrating moment on the course. When you find yourself cursing over the hole you just triple-bogeyed or beating yourself up over hitting another ball OB, you are in the *Fudge* stage. Allow yourself just a brief length of time to be frustrated before you move on to *Fix*. In *Fix*, you have a chance to release your frustration by replacing your negative self-talk with a positive substitute. This could be actually taking another swing, or rehearsing the swing you wanted to make in your mind, or verbally going through the mechanics of a smooth swing, giving you the confidence that you can learn from what you just did and improve your swing. *Forget* is the moment you leave the shot in the past and turn to the next shot. *Focus* is your cue to start thinking about the shot ahead of you: what club you will play and your pre-shot routine.[30]

Can you think of a time when you could have used this method to leave a frustrating moment in the past, imprint a positive replacement, and move forward to the next shot? What specific cues might you use to remind yourself to follow each of these steps?

_____

_____

_____

_____

Countering. All the positive statements and thought changing in the world won't help if you continue to believe the negative thoughts. If you consistently have negative thoughts, you have to attack the root of the negative thought to gain control over your thoughts. By using countering, you develop a defense, based on facts and reason, to do away with the negative thoughts.[31]

Countering is essentially a court case you hold with yourself inside your head. The negative thoughts are the prosecution (the one doing the accusing: "I am not a good golfer."), and you are the defense (the one trying to prove that the positive is true). It is your job to come up with as much factual evidence as you can to disprove the negative thought. The more evidence you bring, or the better the case you develop, the more likely the judge (yourself) will accept and believe the defense. To find evidence, you must do some introspective questioning to discover the root of your thoughts. From the preceding example, if you always think, "I am not a good golfer," you need to step back and ask yourself, "Why do I think this?" and "What evidence is there that can make me change my mind?" A counter response could be, "I practiced at the range three times this week. I have taken many lessons, and I have been visualizing consistently." If you need a greater defense, perhaps think of a few times you were successful at hitting specific shots in the past.

Keep probing your mind and asking yourself questions until you have developed an argument for why you can be successful at whatever skill it is you are trying to master. As the judge, you also hand down the sentence—you make the call. Weigh the evidence and prove yourself not guilty of giving in to negative thinking![32]

Think back to doubtful thoughts you have had about your ability to successfully perform on the golf course. What defense would you use to counter the negative thoughts? Develop a strong case! Create at least two counters for each negative thought.

NEGATIVE THOUGHT	COUNTERS
_____	_____
_____	_____
_____	_____
_____	_____
_____	_____
_____	_____
_____	_____
_____	_____

TAKE IT TO THE COURSE!

Being confident in your golf game isn't something that always comes easily. Not only is creating a positive mind-set challenging, but maintaining and regaining positive images can also be obstacles to golfers. As with all mental skills, patience and practice are the answer. Confidence grows over time, but only if you put yourself on the course and give yourself the opportunity to defeat the negative mind. When you play a round that is particularly positive, take the time to secure that round in your mind by imagining it again, strengthening the muscle memory. Write down the keys to your positive mind that day. Build on the feeling of confidence that comes from a successful day like this, and allow the cycle to continue in a positive manner.

When you do have that ideal day on the course, write down specific positive thoughts or images you had that propelled you through each hole.

_____

_____

_____

_____

SUMMARY

→ Your *perception* of your ability to be successful is foundational to your self-confidence. You have to truly believe in your ability.

→ Your thoughts and beliefs about your ability influence how you feel, which in turn impacts how you play the game. The result of how you play influences your thoughts and beliefs and perpetuates the cycle.

→ Developing consistently good performances starts with developing consistently positive thoughts.

→ There are multiple ways to achieve consistently positive self-talk, including replacing the negative thought with a positive image, thought stopping, thought changing, countering, and affirmation. Remember, positive thinking is a *skill*, and it takes practice.

The path to peak performance isn't necessarily an easy one, but if you believe, you can achieve! Thinking positively will take you many, many miles down the path.

HOW FAR HAVE YOU COME?

The questions in this section are designed to assess how far you have come in applying the techniques of this chapter and what you can work on to improve your confidence. After you have completed the questions and exercises in the Third Hole and practiced some of the self-confidence-enhancing techniques, complete this section.

1. What techniques have you tried to promote an increase in your confidence?

_____

_____

_____

_____

_____

_____

2. Which methods are most effective for you?

_____

_____

_____

_____

_____

_____

3. How has your confidence changed since implementing thought-control techniques?

_____

_____

_____

_____

_____

_____

4. Are you working on replacing negative expectations with positive affirmations? Recall three examples of doing so.

_____

_____

_____

_____

_____

_____

5. In what areas of your game do you still lack confidence? What do you plan to do to change that?

_____

_____

_____

_____

_____

_____

6. Reward yourself for getting this far! Take the time to pat yourself on the back and recognize your efforts in enhancing your mental toughness. Congratulations!

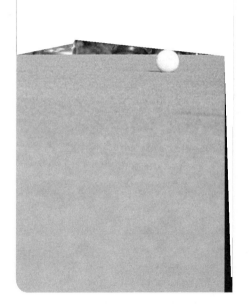

*Consistency
Under Pressure*

magine the pressure Bobby Jones was under as he sought to become the first and only winner of golf's coveted Grand Slam in 1930. The growing crowd was on edge, knowing the importance of this historic event. Beside the demands he put on himself, he felt pressure from his parents, the media, his hometown, and golf fans around the world. At the same time, he battled an illness that left him physically trembling, weak, and often bent double with intense stomach pain.

Yet his concentration on each shot in each round of each tournament was incredible. He rarely wavered or missed a putt. He was able to block out distractions and visualize one shot at a time, reading each lie and following through with his pre-shot plan. When a shot did go slightly awry, he controlled his emotions and moved on to focus entirely on the next shot. For each round he played, in becoming Grand Slam champion, he maintained composure and concentration on the end goal, while directing his mental energy to the shot before him. When reflecting on his U.S. Amateur Open win, the final tournament needed to achieve his dream, Jones said, "I did make plans for that golfing year with precisely this end in view."

TEEING OFF

Bobby Jones's experiences in this game are a great example of how nervousness can be controlled and composure maintained under intense pressure. At one point or another, all players deal with situations like this—although the cause of pressure is often less important than becoming Grand Slam champ. You've most likely experienced tension that caused your mind and body to go haywire and wondered what you could do to perform positively under pressure. Fortunately, you can learn to control the way you respond to the pressures you feel when playing golf.

This chapter helps you:

→ become aware of how and why you act nervously
→ identify the characteristics and influencing factors of nervousness
→ discover techniques to adjust your mental energy levels
→ learn how to consistently turn nervous energy into positive performances
→ become aware of the triggers of peak performance
→ concentrate under pressure
→ avoid the choking danger zone
→ refocus after a concentration lapse or between shots
→ take it to the course

Think for a minute about your last round of golf. What did you remember about the way you were feeling and thinking before and during the round? How did you feel and what were you thinking the night before playing? How about one hour before the start? How did this feeling change ten minutes, five minutes, and one minute before starting? Working through this chapter will improve your awareness of yourself and help you refine your control over your mind and body.

FEELING NERVOUS?

It's only natural to be nervous before playing. Being nervous shows that you care about the outcome and that you believe you have the potential to do well. Unless you scored a 1 on Self-Assessment Scorecard question 13, the trick is to learn to harness your nerves and to use them to your advantage. Visualization is one way to consistently perform well under pressure.

The following list highlights some of the effects you may experience when nervous:[1]

→ increased heart rate
→ increased blood pressure
→ increased respiration rate
→ increased perspiration
→ increased urination frequency
→ increased muscle tension
→ insomnia
→ butterflies in stomach
→ nausea
→ nervous movements
→ narrowing of attention
→ focus on irrelevant cues
→ slower processing of information
→ worry
→ fear
→ doubt
→ negative thoughts about performance
→ difficulty concentrating
→ indecision
→ apprehension
→ disrupted attention
→ decreased sense of well-being

→ decreased sense of control
→ decreased self-confidence
→ expectation of failure

Consider this list and with these things in mind, answer the following questions about yourself.

Do you often experience a great deal of nervousness before or during play? Refer to Self-Assessment Scorecard question 22. With which elements from this list can you identify?

_____

_____

_____

_____

Many factors influence the amount of excitement or nervousness that you as an athlete experience. Some of these factors may include:

→ importance of round or tournament
→ how prepared you feel
→ how skilled you think you are
→ course difficulty
→ weather
→ equipment
→ injuries
→ expectations
→ sight of competitors
→ uncertainty of outcome
→ difficulty of what you are doing
→ obstacles in way of goals (physical and mental)
→ time to think between shots

Knowing what types of situations trigger increased nervousness is key to learning how to control your mind and body. Therefore, a thoughtful response to the next set of questions is important.

Consider the times when your nerves got the better of you. Can you identify the characteristics of those situations that prompted the negative, anxious mind-set? Which of the factors from the previous list played a role? Were there additional factors that triggered your increased nervousness? Write your observations here.

Getting a Grip on Your Nerves

Naturally, when you are feeling too nervous, you want to learn how to clear your mind, calm the butterflies in your stomach, and concentrate on the next shot. On the other hand, if you arrive at the course lacking energy, feeling too relaxed, and thinking about things that are happening off the course, you may need to sharpen your focus and increase your attention. Table 4.1 on the next page lists various techniques you can try to regulate your mental energy.

These simple tricks are quick, are easy, and intuitively make sense. Unfortunately, a quick fix often does not work against serious anxiety and nervousness. Taking time to establish and foster a few of the skills like imagery, goal setting, positive self-talk, and thought control, elaborated on in other chapters of this book, can really help control your mental and physical energy, excitement, and nerves. The key to all of these techniques that regulate nerves is that they can work to build confidence in your ability to perform well and therefore reduce anxiety.

The exercises that follow are specifically designed to help regulate tension. Imagery is one of the most effective for reducing tension or controlling nervousness, as well as for increasing your activation level. Your body will relax in response to peaceful thoughts and prepare for action with energizing thoughts.

> The big trick in putting is not method—the secret of putting is domination of the nerves.
>
> —HENRY COTTON[2]

Relaxing Imagery Script. Begin by taking three abdominal breaths. Listen to the sound of your breathing to block out distracting sounds around you. Now create a picture on the inside of your eyelids of the place in the world where you feel most relaxed, calm, and carefree. Perhaps it's a tropical beach, lying in a hammock, with a gentle breeze

TABLE 4.1 *Techniques for Mental Energy Regulation*[3,4]

Increase Mental Activation	Increase Mental Relaxation
→ Energizing imagery (Try this technique first.)	→ Relaxing imagery (Try this technique first.)
→ Quick, shallow breathing	→ Stretching/Yoga
→ Precompetitive warm-up (exercise)	→ Precompetitive warm-up (exercise)
→ Pep talks	→ Controlled breathing
→ Energizing self-talk	→ Progressive muscle relaxation
→ Goal setting	→ Meditation
→ Music (high-energy)	→ Music (relaxing)
→ Videos (action, inspiring)	→ Negative thought stopping
→ Clapping	→ Focusing on what you can control
→ Using a loud voice	→ Thinking about successes you have had in the past
	→ Keeping things in perspective

blowing over you. Or maybe you imagine a pristine mountaintop with endless views of the clouds below. It could even be as simple as your comfy living room couch or your favorite recliner.

Wherever your "happy place" is, go there now and try to create as many sensory details as possible. Imagine the sights, sounds, feelings, and even tastes and smells. Allow yourself to be in this space, taking in your surroundings as you grow more and more relaxed.

Spend two to five minutes enjoying this solace and gradually come back to your present surroundings, keeping with you the sense of relaxation and calm. Take a few more slow, deep breaths as you return to the here and now. Anytime you need to relax in the future, you may use this technique to help you achieve a more relaxed, present state of mind.

The previous technique is designed to help you reduce tension. The following exercise is one you can use if you are feeling too complacent and in need of a recharge.

Energizing Imagery Script. Use this script if you are feeling flat, have had a bad day, or are feeling down and need a pick-me-up before you head out to the course. Begin by spending fifteen seconds taking quick, shallow breaths to get your adrenaline flowing and to clear your mind. Visualize yourself breathing in energy.

Picture yourself in an exciting round of golf where you are in the lead and a large crowd is cheering your every shot. You absorb their positive energy and feel it coursing through your body. Imagine that your muscles are fired up, coiled up tightly, ready to spring into action. See and feel yourself performing some quick stretches like arm circles, knee lifts, and neck rolls. Perhaps you keep a journal in your golf bag with motivational quotes. Imagine reading these quotes to get yourself pumped up to play.

What other exercises help you become more energized? List and describe them here.

KEEPING THINGS IN PERSPECTIVE

Tom

Golf builds tension. We grip the club tightly on big shots, we get extremely nervous, it's just *such a big deal.* I think it is important to keep golf in perspective. That is, it's not life and death. It's a game, and one you should enjoy. Even the greatest pros of all time have all been on record as saying they played the game because they loved it, not because they had to or because they wanted to become rich and famous. Golfers at all levels, but particularly competitive golfers, hinder their visualization abilities by not keeping golf in perspective.

I have a brother who in big pressure situations always says: "There are a billion people in China who really don't care what I do on this shot." And this relaxes him. Larry Nelson, who won numerous PGA events and two or three majors, didn't pick up the game until he was in his twenties, after a stint in Vietnam. I know he has referenced that experience as real pressure, as opposed to a six-footer for par. I know that having two wonderful kids has really helped my overall composure and ability to remain calm and visualize, because at the end of the round, I know I'm going home to something that is going to blow any golf completely out of the water.

Next are some additional tension-reduction techniques to complement the imagery scripts. You can use these exercises to help achieve your goals from Self-Assessment Scorecard question 24.

Controlled Breathing. There are different ways for you to get air in and out of your lungs. First, you can breathe shallowly and only from your chest. This shallow, chest-level breathing is what people spend most of their time doing. It is also used when you are highly excited or nervous. Second, you can breathe more fully and deeply from the abdomen. This method is called abdominal breathing and is associated with relaxation.[5]

Abdominal breathing exercises are highly recommended as a way to stimulate relaxation in your brain and body.[6] Although chest-level breathing does not have the health benefits of abdominal breathing, it can be used in a controlled way to increase excitement, just as abdominal breathing can be used to decrease it.

> You must swing smoothly to play golf well. And you must be relaxed to swing smoothly.
>
> —BOBBY JONES[7]

The following script leads you through abdominal breathing and calming breath exercises. Read through the script one time. Then practice the skill while you read the script a second time. Study the process so you can try a set or two on your own. At first, practice these skills on a regular basis away from the sport environment, such as when you are lying in your bed before going to sleep. Then once you have mastered the skill, you can incorporate shorter versions into your workouts and competitions. You can do your favorite exercise as part of your pre-shot routine or between shots if you are feeling anxious or nervous.

Abdominal Breathing Exercise. Often referred to as "belly breaths," these specific deep breaths calm your nerves and allow you to refocus. Most of us normally take a deep breath up in our chests. Try it and you'll likely see your chest and shoulders rise on the inhale, fall on the exhale. Abdominal breathing takes place much lower in your body, and that's what has the calming effect. Breathing up in your chest can actually have the opposite result, activating rather than relaxing you. This exercise guides you through abdominal breathing.

1. Note the level of tension you're feeling. Then place one hand on your abdomen (belly) right beneath your rib cage.
2. Inhale slowly and deeply through your nose into the "bottom" of your lungs—in other words, send the air as low down as you can. If you're breathing from your abdomen, your hand should actually rise. Your chest should move only slightly while your abdomen expands. (In abdominal breathing, the diaphragm—the muscle that separates the lung cavity from the abdominal cavity—moves downward. In so doing, it causes the muscles surrounding the abdominal cavity to push outward, causing the stomach to move outward.)
3. When you've taken in a full breath, pause for a moment and then exhale slowly through your nose or mouth, depending on your preference. Be sure to exhale fully. As you exhale, allow your whole body to just let go (you might visualize your arms and legs going loose and limp like a rag doll).
4. Do ten slow, full abdominal breaths. Try to keep your breathing *smooth* and *regular*, without gulping in a big breath or letting your breath out all at once. Remember to pause briefly at the end of each inhalation. Count to ten, progressing with each exhalation. The process should go like this:

   Slow inhale . . . pause . . . slow exhale (count "one")

   Slow inhale . . . pause . . . slow exhale (count "two")

   Slow inhale . . . pause . . . slow exhale (count "three")

   and so on up to ten. If you start to feel light-headed while practicing abdominal breathing, stop for thirty seconds and then start up again.
5. Extend the exercise, if you wish, by doing two to three "sets" of abdominal breaths, remembering to count up to ten for each set (each exhalation counts as one number). Five full minutes of abdominal breathing will have a pronounced effect in reducing your level of excitement.[8]

Some people prefer to count backward from ten down to one on each breath. Feel free to do this if you prefer. At the end of the exercise, you should feel "quieter." It should be easier for you to hold one idea in your mind with fewer distractions. Your muscles should feel more relaxed, and you should be able to stand taller with your shoulders low and your chest high. Your goal in abdominal breathing is to lower your heart rate, clear your mind, and prepare your body for action. Once you get the hang of it, you can use abdominal breathing in briefer doses, one or two breaths at a time, as needed.

Calming Breath Exercise. The calming breath exercise was adapted from the ancient discipline of yoga and was described in part in an earlier chapter.[9] It is a great technique for achieving a deep state of relaxation quickly.

1. Breathing from your abdomen, inhale slowly to a count of five (count slowly "one . . . two . . . three . . . four . . . five" as you inhale).
2. Pause and hold your breath to a count of five.
3. Exhale slowly, through your nose or mouth, to a count of five (or more if it takes you longer). Be sure to exhale fully.
4. When you've exhaled completely, take two breaths in your normal rhythm; then repeat steps 1 through 3 in the preceding cycle.
5. Keep up the exercise for at least five minutes. This should involve going through at least ten cycles of "in five," "hold five," "out five." Remember to take two normal breaths between each cycle. If you start to feel lightheaded while practicing this exercise, stop for thirty seconds and then start again.
6. Throughout the exercise, keep your breathing smooth and regular, without gulping in breaths or breathing out suddenly.
7. Optional: each time you exhale, you may wish to say "Relax," "Calm," "Let go," or any other relaxing word or phrase silently to yourself. Allow your whole body to let go as you do this.

Progressive Muscle Relaxation. Progressive muscle relaxation (PMR) was developed by Dr. Edmund Jacobson as a "systematic technique for achieving a deep state of relaxation."[10] Briefly discussed in an earlier chapter as well, the technique stemmed from Dr. Jacobson's belief that "An anxious mind cannot exist in a relaxed body." Not only is PMR effective at creating immediate relaxation, but if practiced daily for a month or two, it also has the long-term benefit of generalized relaxation throughout the rest of the day.[11]

For best relaxation results with PMR, follow this set of guidelines:

1. Practice every day for at least twenty minutes.
2. Choose a place that is quiet, free of distractions, and comfortable in temperature and lighting.

3. Establish a consistent time to do PMR.
4. Practice on an empty stomach, as deeper relaxation can be achieved when digestion is not occurring.
5. Sit down or lie on your back, whichever is more comfortable.
6. Remove restrictive clothing so you are comfortable.

PMR involves a series of contracting and relaxing exercises targeting all the major muscle groups of the body. Each contraction is held for ten seconds and relaxation is held for fifteen to twenty seconds, giving you time to become fully aware of how it feels to be tense versus how it feels to be relaxed. Maintain your focus on the targeted muscle group. Each time you do a contraction, tighten the specified muscles as hard as you can without hurting yourself, while keeping the rest of the body relaxed. Then release the contraction abruptly and allow full relaxation. If a muscle group is particularly tight, contract and relax it two or three times before moving on.

The following is the detailed script for the PMR technique. You can read through it to learn the muscle sequence and then perform it from memory, including the counting of seconds. Or you can record the script on an audiotape to play back to yourself or buy a professionally made tape to play.

1. To begin, close your eyes. Take three deep abdominal breaths, exhaling slowly each time. As you exhale, imagine that tension throughout your body begins to flow away.
2. Clench your fists. Hold for ten seconds, and then release for fifteen to twenty seconds. Use the same time intervals for all other muscle groups.
3. Tighten your biceps by drawing your forearms up toward your shoulder and "making a muscle" with both arms. Hold . . . and then relax.
4. Tighten your triceps—the muscles on the undersides of your upper arms—by extending your arms out straight and locking your elbows. Hold . . . and then relax.
5. Tense the muscles in your forehead by raising your eyebrows as far as you can. Hold . . . and then relax. Imagine your forehead muscles becoming smooth and limp as they relax.
6. Tense the muscles around your eyes by clenching your eyelids shut. Hold . . . and then relax. Imagine sensations of deep relaxation spreading all around the area of your eyes.
7. Tighten your jaw by opening your mouth so widely that you stretch the muscles around the hinges of your jaw. Hold . . . and then relax. Let your lips part and allow your jaw to hang loose.

8. Tighten the muscles in the back of your neck by pulling your head way back, as if you were going to touch your head to your back (be gentle with this muscle group to avoid injury). Focus on tensing only the muscles in your neck. Hold . . . and then relax. Since this area is often especially tight, it's a good idea to do the tense-relax cycle twice.

9. Take a few deep breaths, and tune in to the weight of your head sinking into whatever surface it is resting on.

10. Tighten your shoulders by shrugging them up as if you were going to touch your ears. Hold . . . and then relax.

11. Tighten the muscles around your shoulder blades by pushing your shoulder blades back as if you were trying to touch them together. Hold the tension in your shoulder blades . . . and then relax. Since this area is often especially tense, you might repeat the tense-relax sequence twice.

12. Tighten the muscles of your chest by taking in a deep breath. Hold for up to ten seconds . . . and then release slowly. Imagine any excess tension in your chest flowing away with the exhalation.

13. Tighten your stomach muscles by sucking your stomach in. Hold . . . and then relax. Imagine a wave of relaxation spreading through your abdomen.

14. Tighten your lower back by arching it up. (You can omit this exercise if you have lower back pain.) Hold . . . and then relax.

15. Tighten your buttocks by pulling them together. Hold . . . and then relax. Imagine the muscles in your hips going loose and limp.

16. Squeeze the muscles in your thighs all the way down to your knees. You will probably have to tighten your hips along with your thighs, since the thigh muscles attach to the pelvis. Hold . . . and then relax. Feel your thigh muscles smoothing out and relaxing completely.

17. Tighten your calf muscles by pulling your toes toward you (flex carefully to avoid cramps). Hold . . . and then relax.

18. Tighten your feet by curling your toes downward. Hold . . . and then relax.

19. Mentally scan your body for any residual tension. If a particular area remains tense, repeat one or two tense-relax cycles for that group of muscles.

20. Now imagine a wave of relaxation slowly spreading throughout your body, starting at your head and gradually penetrating every muscle group all the way down to your toes.

21. Take three more deep abdominal breaths, exhaling slowly each time, before opening your eyes slowly.

Once you have mastered the full-length PMR process, you can use an abbreviated PMR procedure, which combines muscle groups. You can combine contractions of the arm muscles, then facial muscles, then trunk muscles, and then leg muscles, for instance. Remember to continue to tense for ten seconds, relax for fifteen to twenty seconds, and focus on how your body feels.

The key to learning any of these tension-control skills and for ensuring effectiveness is regular practice! So incorporate practice of these skills into your daily and weekly schedules. To begin, select a few skills that you want to try. Practice each skill every day for a week, and then stick with the one you find most effective and enjoyable. Ideally, you'll be able to try all of the exercises to determine the ones that work best for you as an individual.

Make your practice schedule now, and note how helpful each skill is for you.

SKILL	TIME OF DAY	EFFECTIVENESS

Once you've determined a couple of techniques that work well, consider how you might begin to incorporate them into actual play. Be specific about the circumstances on the course where you will use each strategy.

COACH'S CORNER

Instructing your players to "relax" can make them even more tense. Try giving them one of these abbreviated relaxation techniques instead:

→ Breathe deeply from the bottom of the lungs.
→ Repeat the positive mental mantra or swing thought.
→ Visualize feeling calm and swinging smoothly.

Giving them an action item to focus on takes their mind away from distracting thoughts that could otherwise make them tense.

TRIGGERING PEAK PERFORMANCE

The preceding techniques will be easier to apply on the driving range or in casual play, but when the pressure's on, it's a whole different game. One of the areas most negatively affected by the stress of competition is your ability to concentrate. To effectively concentrate when the heat is on, it is vital that you learn what the relevant and irrelevant elements are for your game. Internal triggers are your own thoughts and feelings that bring about a response within you. External triggers are the things in your environment that grab your attention. You can respond to any stimulus in one of two ways. You can either give your attention to the stimulus, or you can ignore it.

What do you think about, see, feel, hear, even smell or taste when you are playing golf? Make a list of as many triggers as you can.

_____

_____

_____

_____

_____

_____

COACH'S CORNER

Do you ever wonder why your players aren't focusing on the right things? Maybe they don't know what they should be focusing on! Sit down with your athletes, either individually or as a team, and talk to them about what specific things they need to be paying attention to during practices and performance. Discuss specific situations so that your athletes will be prepared to deal with anything and everything that comes their way!

Certain things that grab your attention may actually get in the way of your concentration, while others help keep you focused. Relevant triggers are the cues that need your attention for you to successfully perform. For golf, relevant stimuli may include your pre-shot imagery, the way your muscles feel as you swing the club, the feel of the grip in your fingers, the sound of the clubface whacking the ball, the sight of the fairway and your target, and the direction of the wind. You may also have a cue word or swing thought, such as, "Through the ball," that you repeat as you address the ball. Additional relevant triggers could be pain felt after straining your back or butterflies in your stomach before a big shot. At any moment, you should have no more than three or four thoughts in your head. Any more than that, and you are in danger of overthinking and underperforming.

Studies comparing novice and elite athletes demonstrate that significant differences in physical ability are not the primary factor explaining performance differences. Rather, one of the distinguishing characteristics of elite athletes is their increased understanding of what the relevant stimuli are for their sport and their greater ability to attend to them.[12] Strive to be the best! Attend to relevant stimuli.

What should you be focusing on before or during a round of golf?

BEFORE

DURING

_____   _____

_____   _____

_____   _____

_____   _____

_____   _____

_____   _____

_____   _____

_____   _____

_____   _____

Irrelevant triggers are those cues that are not important for and may hinder your performance if allowed into your thinking. It is important that you learn how and when to block out these stimuli. One of the greatest concentration obstacles athletes encounter is attending to irrelevant triggers.[13] Sometimes you may attend to these triggers because you do not know what your attention *should* be focused on, because your nerves are on edge. Each of us has things that tend to attract our attention, but we have to decide whether or not we are going to *let them* distract us.[14, 15]

> just get up to the ball and I see it start down the left side of the fairway and kind of slice back to the right, and when I have that picture in my mind, I make my swing . . . I just get up there and see the ball hooking and then make the swing, and the ball hooks.
>
> —*FRED COUPLES*[16]

There are several types of common distractions that you have probably experienced. These irrelevant triggers may be internal (thoughts and feelings) or external (environmental). Distractions in golf may include spectator noise, the weather, your position on the leaderboard, how others in your group are playing, and your performance on the last shot. Negative self-talk, such as, "I can't believe I missed that easy putt," is also a distraction because it prevents you from focusing positively on the next shot.

If you give any stimulus so much attention that you are unaware of or inattentive to relevant triggers, it is a distraction. If your thoughts or feelings, positive or negative, become so much of a focus that they keep you from attending to other relevant triggers, it is a distraction and can inhibit you from performing at your best.[16]

CONCENTRATION UNDER PRESSURE

Your ability to attend to relevant triggers and to ignore distractions is impacted by your level of physical and mental tension.

When mental activation is low, we take in a large number of relevant and irrelevant pieces of information. Because we are taking in too much information, specifically irrelevant information, performance suffers. For example, a player who is mentally flat may notice his girlfriend in the crowd, start planning too many shots in advance, obsess over past poor shots, and other things that are not important to the competition.

At the other end of the spectrum, if activation keeps increasing past the optimal level to high levels, your ability to concentrate will suffer. As your focus becomes more and more narrow, both irrelevant and relevant information will be ignored. Thus performance declines because important triggers like visualization, grip, and breathing, are forgotten. Your play becomes paralyzed.

Consider playing in a tournament where you are so anxious that you are unaware of the firm conditions of greens and therefore fail to compensate adequately with your backspin. Or you may unintentionally select the wrong club and drive the ball significantly short of your target. You don't want to be caught in either of these situations.

Where you do want to be is right in the middle. As mental activation levels, attention narrows and we tend to pick out the information that is relevant to performance and ignore what is distracting. This leveling of attention results in improved performance.

When you are ideally focused, you will be able to block out the distracting noises around you and listen solely for the sound of the club swiftly swinging through the plane of motion and striking the ball. You will be able to perform your pre-shot imagery, manage the course, and choose the correct club for each shot without being preoccupied by your score or standing.

Consider Figure 4.1, which demonstrates the narrowing of attention with increasing activation and the types of cues that receive attention.

FIGURE 4.1 *Model showing the narrowing of attentional focus that occurs with increasing mental activation*[18]

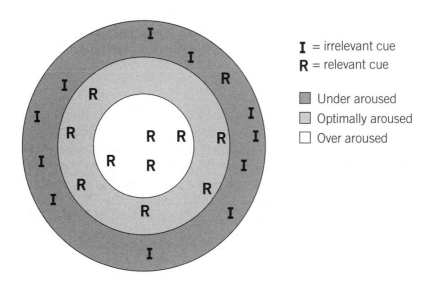

Can you think of times when you focused on things that were not relevant to your golf game? Identify the triggers you focused on in each case.

_____

_____

_____

_____

In similar situations in the future, which triggers most likely will help you maintain proper focus? Be specific.

_____

_____

_____

_____

This optimal level of mental energy is where peak performance tends to occur, because all of the relevant triggers are addressed and all the distractions are ignored. Use the previously described energy-regulation techniques—for example, relaxing imagery—to consistently concentrate and play great golf under pressure.

The Danger Zone

We've all been there. It's the eighteenth hole. You've been shooting the lights out. You are on the green and know that if you can just make this putt for par, you will break ninety for the first time. It's an undulating twenty footer. You go to school, watching the player ahead of you take her shot and try to get a read on the green. Her shot lips out. You eagerly grab your putter, and as you line up your putt, your mind races: "I hope my putt doesn't miss like hers did. I could break my personal record right here, as long as I don't mishit it." You imagine the joy you will feel as your friends all pat you on the back and congratulate you in the clubhouse. You quickly address the ball, pull back the club, and gently strike the ball. As soon as your putter contacts your ball, you know you've mishit it. You've blown the putt five feet by. You can't believe it. Today is not the day for your record-breaking score. Now all you want to do is get the ball in the hole and go home. You end up three putting for ninety-one.

Choking occurs when you're paralyzed by an inability to properly focus. Play deteriorates to the point where it seems there is nothing you can do to regain your form. The player in the preceding example was so caught up in the moment and the excitement of what could be that she did not take the time to prepare as she should have. She should have visualized her shot, taken the time to complete her pre-shot routine, repeated her mental mantra, and remained focused on the present, as she had the previous seventeen holes.

While we cannot completely eliminate choking, we can certainly reduce the frequency of occurrence by adopting the techniques described in this chapter both in practice and competitive pressure situations. Most players don't realize they are choking until after they've blown it. But by tuning in to your relevant triggers, you should be aware of any distractions attacking your game. If you sense that you are starting to choke, focus attentively on your relevant triggers, be they your deep abdominal breathing or the timing of your pre-shot routine.

> As I walked to the eighteenth hole, I let myself get down and failed to think like a champion. Rather than roll up my sleeves and tell myself I was going to birdie the hole to win, I thought about what I didn't want to do. I didn't want to make a bogey. As a result, I made a very scared swing with the driver and blocked it slightly into the right rough . . . I two putted for a bogey.
>
> —PETER JACOBSEN [19]

A NO-FEAR APPROACH

Mary Jo

As a coach, my main job is to help my players play their best and perform at their highest level when it counts. Players can be very different as far as what techniques work to get them there. However, the key element found in all champions is that they are not afraid of winning. As players work on their games and improve during practice, some can actually become *fearful* of success and of playing better than their comfort zone. They become fearful of not being able to bring their practice game to the course or to hit that critical shot under pressure. How many times have you heard someone say, "It's too bad the tournament isn't on the range!"?

That's where it's important to practice more like the game is played and to put pressure on yourself whenever you practice. Just scraping and hitting ball after ball on the range will not significantly improve your game when the pressure is on. You might develop a few better mechanics with your golf swing, but you will not be ready for pressure situations on the course.

It's important to go through your routine on the range. Stand behind your ball, say to yourself, "This is the first hole, and I need to hit my drive between those two spots." Visualize and go. Make believe that you are in the tournament. The more you can visualize and put pressure on yourself in practice, the more you can relax and let go of fear on the course. Your mind will tell you, "Been there, done that—this is easy."

The same holds true for putting. Just practicing with two balls around the practice green is not all that effective. The second ball is usually closer or in! You don't get a second chance to hit another putt from the same spot when you play, so why are you doing that when you practice? It's much more effective to do a putting drill that puts pressure on your putting stroke. For example, play a "nine-hole match" with yourself with one ball when you are on the practice green and see if you score under par (less than two putts per hole for the nine holes).

Keep it real during practice, and you'll experience less fear when your game is under pressure on the course!

Regardless of the final outcome, always try to walk off the course with at least three positive takeaways from the round, however small they may be. This way you will always look forward to coming back stronger.

Think about a time when the pressure was on and you choked. How could you have better handled the situation? (Refer back to your answer to question 14 of the Self-Assessment Scorecard. Perhaps that will help you.)

Can you think of three positive aspects of your game that day?

1. _____

   _____

2. _____

   _____

3. _____

   _____

PLAYER'S POINTER

Competition simulation is an incredible tool you can use to become familiar and comfortable with the attentional demands of competition. Try asking a pro to watch you play or playing with a group of players above your level. Also, by frequently visualizing yourself in high-pressure situations—playing against your boss, putting for the win, driving on the final hole of your best round ever—you'll become aware of the competition environment and be better prepared to deal with the associated relevant and irrelevant stimuli.

Refocusing

Once your attention has been taken prisoner, how do you get it back from the enemy of distraction? The first thing to keep in mind is that *you are in control of your reactions.* How you respond to a stimulus determines whether or not something is a distraction. You choose! Poor performances cannot be blamed on distractions, but only on an inability to properly focus.[20] You are not expected to maintain continuous focus throughout an entire round of golf. Rather, it is more effective to focus intensely *just* before each shot and let yourself relax during the in-between times when you do not need to be "on." In a four-hour round of golf, you are playing the ball for only approximately six minutes.[21] Just think of the three hours and fifty-four minutes of mental peace you could enjoy! Releasing yourself from the pressure of four to five hours of overwhelming mental fatigue keeps your mind fresh for the central aspects of the game.

You may also try thinking of each hole as a mini game—a game within a game. Stay focused on the present game (hole), and keep in mind that there is no relationship to how you played the last game and your potential to do well on the current game. Count how many games you "win" as well as calculating your overall score for the round. This may bring a fun change to the way you think about the game, and help you leave the last hole in the past and focus on what is right in front of you.

Again, it is of utmost importance for you to know what the relevant and irrelevant triggers are so you can focus on what is appropriate for the situation. If you do not have an understanding of these, you will not know what to focus on when you do become distracted. Once more, how you react to the situation is in your control. Focusing on what is in your control is key to regaining proper concentration when you are distracted.[22] You can choose to change the way you are thinking or feeling. You can choose to take your attention away from the crowd or the leaderboard or whatever mistake you made and place it on something else. You are in control!

Refer to Self-Assessment Scorecard question 15 to remind you of how well you believe you can refocus under pressure. These refocusing skills can be enhanced by using the concentration techniques described next.

Refocusing Imagery Script. Before you begin this exercise, be sure to take a few deep breaths and relax.

You are playing your favorite course on a beautiful, sunny day and enjoying the round. The next hole is a challenging par-five dogleg right, with water hazards on both sides of the fairway and the back of the green. You have been shooting a great round and feeling like you are playing in the zone. But you just four-putted the last hole and that broke your concentration and rhythm. You approach the sixteenth hole frustrated and thinking negatively.

What are you going to do? What strategies will you use to bring your attention to this next shot? How will you block out the negative result of the previous shot and refocus yourself? Use these questions to complete the following script.

_____

_____

_____

_____

_____

_____

_____

_____

_____

_____

Competition Simulations. Use this technique to help improve your ability to block out distractions.[23, 24] It is easy to become so aware of the typical triggers surrounding your golf game that the irrelevant stimuli are no longer distracting. This is achieved by simulating the actual competition environment as closely as possible in practice. It is important to practice a variety of different possible competition situations on the driving range. Pretend you are playing out an entire hole on the driving range. First you drive to the fairway; then you take your approach shot with your 5-iron. What hazards did you visualize? Where were the trees, the bunker, the water? Where was your imagined target? Did you hit it? Every time you go to the driving range, visualize yourself playing actual holes. This competition simulation convinces your brain that you have "been there, done that," giving you the confidence you need to perform under pressure the next time you are on the course.

Other examples of competition simulations include visually blocking out other golfers at the driving range as you would spectators and your competitors on the course, playing on wet grass, or imagining pressure situations. By practicing like this, you learn to ignore distractions. Performance becomes second nature, reducing the newness and unfamiliarity of actual competitive situations.

Describe the elements you would include in your own competition simulations. What competition distractions can you simulate at the driving range or on the course? What different specific scenarios could be practiced?

_____

_____

_____

_____

_____

Attentional Cues. Use this exercise to help improve your focus on the important parts of your game and to help refocus once your concentration is broken.[25, 26]

Verbal, visual, and kinesthetic cues can be very useful in helping you regain lost concentration or guide your focus in the appropriate direction. By using cues, irrelevant stimuli are pushed aside and the relevant cues dominate. Cues break down a movement, highlighting where attention should be focused for the specific task. Cue words should focus on *positives*, the *present*, and the *process*.

Verbal cues remind you of what to focus on. You may use a swing thought such as "Strong and smooth." Kinesthetic cues focus attention the way the movement feels, such as picturing yourself holding a club made of glass. This reminds you to maintain a gentle grip throughout your swing. Another example may be to feel as if you have long arms as you swing the club through freely.

A great example of visual cues is the triple threat series of lie, distance, and trajectory. You can quickly remember this as LDT, a simple visual trigger that cues your mind to focus on three important aspects of the shot: the *l*ie of the ball, the *d*istance to the next target, and the *t*rajectory you need.[27] Focusing on these three visual cues helps you block out distractions and stay positive.

A combination of verbal, visual, and kinesthetic cues will effect improved performance if practiced regularly.

COACH'S CORNER

Work with your athletes to develop and use appropriate and personalized attentional cues. Encourage your players to practice concentration exercises and incorporate them in between drills during practice.

Plan—identify cue words you think would help you in your golf performances. Indicate the specific situations in which you would use them:

CUE WORD	SITUATION
1. _____	_____
2. _____	_____
3. _____	_____
4. _____	_____

5. _____ _____

6. _____ _____

Focus and Refocus. These two techniques are used to regain lost concentration and composure.[28] They teach you to maintain concentration in the present, without being distracted by past mistakes or future worries. To be successful, you must be able to get rid of negative or distracting thoughts and focus concentration entirely in the here and now. Try these two exercises for five minutes each day, noting improvements as you continue. Lengthen time as concentration improves.

→ **Mindfulness.** Sit quietly in a comfortable position, close your eyes, and see how long you can hold one thought in your head before becoming distracted. When you are distracted, regain the thought and try again. The thought can be anything, golf-related or not. Just pick a thought and stick with it.

→ **One-Point Focus.** Find an object representing golf, whether it be a ball, club, glove, tee, or a photograph of a player in action. Look at the object, focusing only on it. When distracting thoughts come to mind, bring your attention back to the object. This will be challenging, so continue to practice, knowing that it's helping your game.

COURSE MANAGEMENT

One of the biggest pressures players face is deciding the type of shot and distance you need to hit your target, which club is best for that shot, and how to properly execute the shot. Is your pitching wedge going to put you too far from the pin? Should you use the gap wedge instead? Does it have enough loft to get you in good position? How far are you from the pin? Will a fairway wood give you the distance you need off the tee? In a situation where you have a challenging decision to make, weigh your odds and make the choice. Then stick with your decision with 100 percent commitment.

> Relax. Enjoy the walk between shots. That's your chance to loosen up so your next shot is comfortable.
>
> —*JULIUS BOROS*[29]

Whether or not you *actually* made the right choice is less important than your belief in your choice. If, when you address the ball with your

3-wood, you are still mentally debating the benefits of using your driver, you are *not* thinking about the stroke you are about to make with your 3-wood. Thus your concentration is not sharp, and the resulting shot will probably disappoint you.

To help you stick to your choice and forget the alternatives, you may visualize the chosen shot, repeat your mental mantra, and rely on your cues. All of these actions change your focus from the analytical, mentally wrangling to the decisive, clearheaded player you want to be.

TAKE IT TO THE COURSE!

Playing in intimidating situations can be a significant challenge. Take, for instance, a scenario in which you are playing for the first time with your boss or with a client whose business you are trying to secure. Or consider trying to qualify for the state championship. Perhaps you have entered a Pro-Am tournament with players well above your level.

Think of other circumstances under which you have played that create such an intense pressure, nervousness, and an anxious desire to play well.

_____

_____

_____

_____

Situations such as these can create intense nervousness and make it difficult to play your best. Stick to your mental game plan to block out distractions and focus on the relevant triggers.

Which techniques, as described in this chapter, will you use to help overcome this nervousness? (For example, PMR, deep breathing, or relaxation imagery.)

_____

_____

_____

_____

_____

COACH'S CORNER

As an instructor, you should be aware that you may use strategies that inadvertently increase player's nerves. Table 4.2 lists some common coaching practices and some more effective alternatives.

TABLE 4.2 *Coaching Strategies*[30]

Common Practices	Effective Alternatives
→ Teaching right before or during the competition	→ Practice time is for teaching; during competition, trust that your players have absorbed your instruction.
→ Making pressure statements, such as, "You have to birdie this hole," or "You're three shots back."	→ Simply focus on the positives, such as reminding them to use their pre-shot routines and to visualize each shot.
→ Using criticism as a motivator	→ Positive reinforcement works better because it allows players to focus on what they can control, rather than instilling fear of negative outcomes.
→ Using negative statements, such as "Don't hit into the water."	→ Serve your ideas on a silver platter. Using positive instruction allows a player to take immediate action, rather than to first convert a negative to a positive. Say, "Hit it onto the green."
→ Setting unattainable goals	→ Realistic goals foster the strongest motivation. See Chapter 5 for details.
→ Inducing guilt over poor performances	→ Ask your players to write down three good things from every performance, even if they are small.
→ Blaming others for mistakes	→ Remind your athletes to focus on the things they can control, rather than using others as excuses for poor play.

SUMMARY

→ Nervousness is natural, and the key to success is learning to control it through mental techniques. Many factors affect the intensity of nerves.

→ You can control your nerves using mental energy regulation with techniques such as calming breath, abdominal breathing, PMR, and imagery.

→ Understanding relevant and irrelevant triggers is key to concentrating under pressure.

→ Choking can be reduced by taking the time to focus on the relevant elements.

→ To refocus, try competition simulation, attentional cues, mindfulness, and one-point focus. You are in control of your reaction to pressure.

You have the ability to create the optimal mental energy level for your performances. The tools presented in this chapter should put you well on your way to consistently creating this ideal performance zone, better enabling you to experience peak performances.

HOW FAR HAVE YOU COME?

The questions in this section are designed to assess how far you have come in applying the techniques of this chapter and what you can work on to improve your ability to control tension. Wait until you have had a chance to practice mental energy control techniques and have addressed all the questions in the Fourth Hole chapter before completing this section.

1. Describe your typical performance in terms of symptoms of excitement and nervousness prior to your work with this chapter.

_____

_____

_____

_____

_____

_____

2. Which energy-controlling techniques have you tried? Under what conditions?

_____

_____

_____

_____

_____

_____

3. Which technique(s) do you like best in terms of ease and effectiveness?

_____

_____

_____

_____

_____

_____

4. What changes have you noticed in your mental tension level before and during competitive play?

_____

_____

_____

_____

_____

_____

5. Do you feel more in control of your mind and body? Explain.

_____

_____

_____

_____

_____

_____

6. What needs further work? Which other techniques might you try? Do you need to dedicate more time to practicing these?

_____

_____

_____

_____

_____

_____

7. Reward yourself for getting this far! Take the time to pat yourself on the back and to recognize your efforts in enhancing your mental toughness. Congratulations!

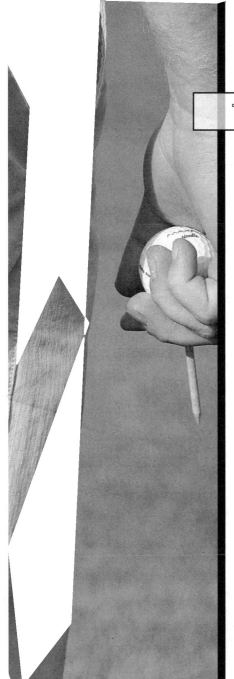

5

*Your Internal
Driver*

S ix months ago, Sarah, a college freshman, joined the golf team with the hopes of staying fit, meeting new friends and playing the sport she has loved for ten years. Since she joined the team, her experiences have been tremendous. New information caught and held her attention throughout the fall season. The coaches had new techniques to show her, and the school's home course is a challenging one. Being part of a team was a whole new experience, as she had been used to practicing on her own local course. The demands of leadership and teamwork on a college team were not only invigorating, but also enlightening. She discovered a great deal about the way she learns and the way she interacts with others. She also had the opportunity to be outside, which was an especially welcome respite from all the demands of classes.

Now, however, the team has started their indoor winter training. Gone are the days of sunshine and fresh air. The team no longer meets as a group. Instead, they are asked to go to the weight room on their own to complete physical workouts designed to build strength and flexibility. The requirements have become much harder each month. She feels tired all the time and misses having more free time. The excitement she once had about going to practice has diminished. All that seems to be left is the drudgery of going to the gym and the indoor putting areas. Although Sarah made a commitment to herself and to her teammates to participate throughout the winter and spring seasons, she feels little motivation to go to practice, let alone to train hard once she gets there.

TEEING OFF

Whether it is to perform better than others, compete against yourself, strive to be the best you can be, be part of a social network, learn a new skill, make friends, attain the status afforded by our society to golfers, or simply to have fun, you likely start off each season with motivation. Sometimes, however, like Sarah from the previous anecdote, you may find it difficult to maintain this motivation as the years of participation go by, as the season continues, or even through a bad round. Often players look within themselves and to coaches, competition, rewards, teammates, and even to higher powers to find the drive to continue an activity that once was fun but has since become a chore.

The goal of this chapter is to come up with a usable framework under which you can:

→ identify how you are motivated
→ understand why some players take action while others slack off, and become one who consistently gives full effort
→ discover the controllables and uncontrollables on the course
→ establish a M.A.S.T.E.R. goal-setting program that helps you maintain and even increase the kind of motivation you need to succeed in golf
→ create your own specific goal achievement plan to help you achieve your golf ambitions

THE DRIVE TO SUCCEED

Motivation is the force that energizes and directs athletic behavior.[1] It is the reason why we do what we do, and *every* action a person takes is a result of some form of motivation.[2] Motivation can come in two forms: intrinsic and extrinsic. Intrinsic motivation comes from within you and drives you to persist. Golfers who have fun and experience satisfaction in reaching and surpassing their own personal potential through training are intrinsically motivated. Extrinsic motivation is derived from any outside source that provides a reason for you to continue to play. Players who perform to receive a reward or to avoid embarrassment employ extrinsic motivation.[3] More examples of intrinsic and extrinsic motivators are given in Table 5.1.

TABLE 5.1 *Examples of Intrinsic and Extrinsic Motivators*

Intrinsic Motivators	Extrinsic Motivators
→ Satisfaction from working hard	→ Money
→ Excitement of participation	→ Titles
→ Love of the game	→ Approval of others
→ Desire to overcome obstacles	→ Fear of losing
→ Joy of being around teammates	→ Peer pressure

Which Type Is Best?

Rarely are athletes entirely extrinsically motivated or entirely intrinsically motivated. Some sport psychology experts would actually argue that no one ever experiences absolute intrinsic motivation; we will always receive a reward in some form for our participation. This argument aside, however, each player tends to have a personal dominant motivational orientation.

What motivates you to play golf? (Refer to Self-Assessment Scorecard question 17.) What do you enjoy most about the game? Why do you choose to go to the course?

_____

_____

_____

_____

If you were to visualize your perfect day on the course, what elements would it include? Who would be with you? How would you feel? On what golf course would you be playing? What would you hear?

_____

_____

Indicate where you think you fall on the line below:

INTRINSICALLY MOTIVATED   **EXTRINSICALLY MOTIVATED**

←——————————————————————————————→

Although it's OK for athletes to use extrinsic rewards to stimulate motivation, too much of a good thing can be bad. Rewards have been shown to undermine intrinsic motivation, the form of motivation that most influences performance.[5] Extrinsic rewards are not sustainable over a period of time; neither do they allow you to be in control of your game. If you were given twenty dollars every time you set foot on the course, after the initial shock of getting paid, you would become accustomed to the reward. Soon twenty dollars would not be enough. You would want thirty dollars. Eventually, only forty dollars would do, and if you didn't get the money one day, you would certainly be less inclined to play. Your intrinsic motivation to play for the fun of the sport would be undermined by an extrinsic monetary reward.[6] Strengthening intrinsic motivation is essential because focusing on the things you can control is motivating for the long term.

Unfortunately, regardless of this undermining trend, when players feel motivation drop, they try to revive it with extrinsic rewards. You may have heard someone in your foursome try to up the ante by saying something like, "I'll buy you a drink if you sink this putt," or you may have said to yourself, "If I hit the green on this shot, I'm going to buy myself a new driver." In both cases, your focus goes to the reward (the refreshments in the clubhouse or shopping for the new club) and forgets the task at hand (the next shot).

To build up your intrinsic motivation and confidence, it is of utmost importance that you keep your focus on what *you* can control. You are in control of your own performance, but you are *not* in control of how others perform. So you should visualize yourself addressing the ball, smoothly swinging the club back, and squarely impacting the ball on the downswing. This imagery helps you focus on the internal motivators such as the satisfying feeling of a well-hit shot. By strengthening your intrinsic motivation, you may enhance your sense of control over your performance.

Simply staying in touch with your enjoyment of the sport through a tough round or the yips can have a stronger influence on motivation than trying to increase extrinsic motivation. Keep this in mind later in this chapter when we discuss goal setting.

Replaying the visualization script you sketched out in the previous question about your ideal day is a helpful technique that can strengthen your intrinsic motivation. Try it the next time you feel you need a boost.

WHY ARE SOME PEOPLE MOTIVATED WHEN OTHERS ARE NOT?

Take a moment to answer the following two questions:
Recall your worst round in the past few months. Why did it happen?

_____

_____

_____

_____

Recall your best performance. Why did it happen?

_____

_____

_____

Where we attribute our successes and failures influences future play and subsequent motivation.[7] How you explain your success in golf—or lack thereof—is referred to here as an attribution. Examples of attributions include comments like, "I didn't play well because the weather was lousy," "I was successful because I trained harder than anyone else out there today," or "I nailed that putt because I stuck to my pre-shot routine." It's all about your perceptions and interpretations, and these are well within your control. You just need to understand exactly where they come from, and then you can start to take control.

Golfers attribute success and failure to five main areas: ability, effort, task diffi-

> uck? Sure. But only after long practice and only with the ability to think under pressure.
>
> —BABE DIDRIKSON ZAHARIAS[8]

culty, expectations, and luck. Ability refers to how skilled you are at the tasks required in your golf game; effort is how much you put into your game or into practice leading up to the performance. Task difficulty refers to how tough the course, opponents, or conditions are. Expectations refer to the level of play you demand from yourself and the confidence you have in your game. Luck, as we all know, is the uncontrollable influence of fortune, chance, or circumstance.

Look at your answers to the previous two questions. What attributions did you use to explain the worst and best performances of the season?

_____

_____

_____

Generally, where do you find yourself laying blame for poor performances? How do you explain the great ones?

_____

_____

_____

Players often attribute their successes to ability, effort, and expectations. These are internal, controllable characteristics. In contrast, players often attribute their failures to luck and task difficulty, or external, uncontrollable characteristics. When you feel in control of what needs to change to obtain success, and what needs to change is *your own* behavior, then your motivation is strengthened.[9] If, however, you attribute success to luck and lack of task difficulty, and failure to lack of ability and effort, you do not feel in control of what needs to change for your performance to improve. In this case, motivation will diminish in the long run.

Do you believe your attributions are helping improve your game and increase your motivation? If not, how might you change your thinking to take ownership of your success and failures on the course?

_____

_____

Stay in Control

So what's the short answer to finding and maintaining strong motivation? Focus on what you can control! Effort leads to an increase in ability. Ability leads to higher expectations. Higher expectations and confidence help you overcome difficult tasks or a bit of bad luck. This combination leads to lower scores and higher satisfaction. Start by focusing on your effort. You are in control of your effort, and a change in that effort can lead to improved performances. Improved performances should lead to success, even if that success is subjective. A subjectively successful performance is one in which you know you have performed well, although you did not necessarily *win*. Remember how we recommended you take away at least three positive things from every round you play? These successes should help maintain and even increase your motivation to succeed.

What important pre-round or pre-shot preparations can you control in a typical round of golf? What factors are outside of your control?

CONTROLLABLES	UNCONTROLLABLES
1. _____	_____
_____	_____
2. _____	_____
_____	_____
3. _____	_____
_____	_____
4. _____	_____
_____	_____
5. _____	_____
_____	_____
6. _____	_____
_____	_____
7. _____	_____
_____	_____

8. _____   _____

_____   _____

9. _____   _____

_____   _____

10. _____   _____

_____   _____

Think back to a time on the course or practice range when you felt your motivation drop. Write down at least three things you were in control of at that time. Example: positive imagery, mental mantra, deep breathing. Write a short list of cues for you to visualize these controllables to boost your effort.

_____

_____

_____

_____

_____

Often, when you feel your motivation drop, you don't want to put forth any more effort. What positive images, swing thoughts, or activation techniques can you use to help you push through in these critical times?

_____

_____

_____

_____

_____

_____

COACH'S CORNER

When a player's motivation starts to sag, you should jump in and remind her to visualize what she can control on the next shot. Help her create a vivid image by suggesting different sensory cues. Offering this action-oriented thought gives the brain something tangible to focus on, rather than the negatives.

GOAL ACHIEVEMENT STRATEGIES

So what do you do with all this information? The answer to this question is simple: set goals! Goal setting gives you a plan of attack for each practice of each week of each season. Goals transform your big dreams of breaking eighty or playing at Pebble Beach into a tangible plan of action. Researchers have found that goal setting helps improve performance by focusing and directing athletes. Goals build motivation, keep you focused when your game is not going well, increase effort, and help keep your game in perspective. Goals also provide feedback, illustrating where efforts are paying off and where more effort needs to be placed. In short, goals can help establish, maintain, and increase motivation.

Visualizing yourself achieving your goals helps you attain them more quickly. Picturing what it will feel like and look like to keep your head down and to swing through the ball, for example, builds your muscle memory and confidence.

M.A.S.T.E.R. Your Goals

Any old goal will not do, however. Taking the time to adhere to the following criteria will get you much further than just daydreaming about your dream round. Setting M.A.S.T.E.R. goals helps you to become a better golfer:

→ **Measurable.** Create goals so that you can tell when you have reached them. Do not simply say, "I will do my best." It is very difficult to measure exactly what your "best" is, and you may be the only one who knows. "I will spend at least twenty minutes stretching after practice to improve my flexibility," is a far more measurable statement. You can measure twenty minutes, and anyone who watches you can verify whether you spend the extra time on stretching.

→ **Adaptable.** Your goals should be flexible (like your muscles), adapting to the changing needs of each moment, round, and season. A goal of lowering your handicap of nineteen by two may be realistic at the start of the season when you haven't played much, but as you practice and improve, similar reductions become harder and harder to attain. The goal needs to be adjusted accordingly.

→ **Specific.** The more specific your goals, the better. A goal of making more chip shots is good. A goal of successfully chipping twelve out of fifteen shots onto the green by the end of the summer is better. When you think your goal is specific enough, make it even more precise. The more detailed the goal, the more likely it will lead to increased motivation and improved performance.

→ **Time-Bound.** Set a date of achievement for every goal. Having a time frame allows you to check in on your progress and keeps you on track toward success. "I will make twenty-five putts before I leave today," or "I'm going to work up to practicing at the driving range for an hour a day, four days a week, by July first." As the deadline approaches, you are likely to work harder to reach your goal on time, and when the time arrives, you can reward yourself for your accomplishment.

→ **Encouraging.** Be positive! Instead of saying, "I can't make any bogeys on the back nine," say, "I will try to stick to my pre-shot routine so I can make par on the back nine." This is possibly *the most important* element in structuring your goals. Be extra careful to ensure that you write each goal in positive terms.

→ **Realistic.** Set goals that are difficult yet attainable, challenging yet reasonable. An easy goal is boring, and one that is nearly impossible is discouraging. You're likely to strive for a goal that inspires you.

→ **In addition.** Build rewards and reminders into your goal-setting program. Also, "Ink it, don't just think it!"[10] Make sure to write down all your goals to keep them in the forefront of your mind. You may want to keep a goal journal (or even this book) with you in your golf bag. This way, you can refer to your goals if your motivation starts to dip or if you need to be reminded of what you're trying to accomplish and of the success you have already achieved.

Keep in mind that you should set goals that you are in control of attaining. Visualize yourself draining twenty-five putts at the end of practice, making a stroke that feels really great, or hitting your target. Focus on your improved performance as an individual—something you can control. Goals of beating an opponent or driving farther than the others in your group make your success dependent on the acts of others. Since you have no control over anyone but yourself, it makes little sense to hinge your success on how well your performance relates to your competitors' performances. Instead, set goals that focus on your own skills and visualize the steps you need to take to master them.

COACH'S CORNER

Setting goals as a team may be challenging, but when done well, it is worth the effort! There are three phases to a team goal-setting program: the planning, the meeting, and the follow-up phases. In the planning phase, you should identify each player's individual and team needs. In the meeting phase, teach your players about the goal-setting process and determine what they would like to get out of the season. Then set up one-on-one meeting times to go over each of their individual goals. Finally, set aside time weekly for players to check their progress. Schedule goal meetings throughout the season to reevaluate unrealistic goals, provide rewards or positive feedback for accomplished goals, and set new ones.[11]

Goals Assessment

Take a moment to complete the following exercise. The more time you take to give detailed responses, the more you will get out of the exercise.

What do you ultimately want to achieve in golf? What is your biggest dream for yourself as a player? How long do you think it may take to reach this goal? (If you scored a 1 or 2 on question 16 of the Self-Assessment Scorecard, you can probably answer this easily. If not, think hard and be creative.)

_____

_____

_____

_____

_____

While you progress toward that ambition, what other successes do you see yourself achieving in golf?

_____

_____

_____

_____

TAKE IT UP A NOTCH

Tim

I am a forty-one-year-old who has played golf as a hobby for twenty-three years. Prior to that, I played competitively for two years in high school. I have since played five times per year on average, and as a result, I am a bogey golfer. I really enjoy being on the course and playing the game, but I am tired of bogey golf. At the beginning of this year, I decided that my best years of golf can be ahead of me if I'm willing to work at it. So I set some short-term goals to help with motivation. My two goals were to get my handicap into the single digits and to play in at least one tournament. Not too lofty, but motivating, nonetheless.

I started the process by building a custom set of clubs that fit me, found the right ball for my game, and practiced one day a week on the driving range, which is something I've never done. I then retooled my swing, incorporated video analysis, studied trigonometry and physics and its involvement in the golf swing, and purchased a golf GPS unit to remove the guesswork of distance.

I now have two of the most challenging and difficult parts of the game to address ahead of me: course management and the mental game. Both of these will provide the necessary motivation for years to come. I will never master the game, but I'm glad golf is so mentally demanding because it will always keep me engaged and motivated to improve.

What goals do you have for this season? Where do you hope to be at the beginning of next season?

Keeping in mind your goals for this season, set three goals to focus on this week. At least one of these goals should focus on visualization.

1. _____

_____

_____

2. _____

_____

_____

3. _____

_____

_____

COACH'S CORNER

To help players set goals that they can achieve, encourage them to visualize each step. Often, it's tempting to ask them to picture themselves winning. While this is the end goal, it's the intermediate goals that really matter—every bit of preparation, every stroke, every club choice. Make sure your players visualize themselves going through the motions, not just holding the trophy overhead.

Players often go through their day-to-day lives without their long-term expectations in mind. Similarly, your long-term hopes do not always coincide with what you would like to accomplish from day to day. For example, your long-term hope may be to stay fit and healthy, but you may not want to get up early each morning to go to the gym. Coordinating these short- and long-term desires can lead to a clearer progression toward attaining your goals on and off the course. You may apply these goal-achievement tips not only to your golf game, but to work, personal life, and other sports, as well. See Chapter 6, "Life's Lessons," for further discussion about how the mental game plays off the course.

M.A.S.T.E.R. Goals Imagery Script. To really find success with this goal-setting process, it's important to write down your goals. But it's essential to visualize yourself achieving them every step of the way. Look back at the answers you gave earlier regarding your general and specific golf goals; then close your eyes and imagine yourself reaching them. Go through one goal at a time in your mind, visualizing each step you will undertake en route to success. If your long-term goal is to lower your handicap from fifteen to ten, your three goals for this week may be to go to the driving range for two hours on Tuesday evening, to visualize fifty putts and ten drives before you go to bed each night, and to set up a lesson with an instructor over the weekend. Thus you want to visualize yourself succeeding in each of these scenarios. See yourself packing up your clubs, jumping in the car, and driving to the range at six o'clock. Feel each of your fifty putts go in, noting the feel of your grip, your balanced stance, your even stroke, and the sound of contact. Mentally rehearse what you will say when you request a lesson from the pro.

So review the goals you wrote earlier; then see, feel, hear, and even smell and taste yourself following the path to success on each of those positive stepping stones. Visualizing the whole process—not just the end result—is the quickest and most reliable way of achieving your M.A.S.T.E.R. goals.

Setting Your Goals. Goals come in three forms:

Short-term (up to two weeks)

Intermediate (through this season)

Long-term (beyond this season)

Goal setting is a process that uses short-term goals to reach intermediate goals, which eventually fulfill long-term goals. Short-term goals take into account and help you work toward the intermediate and long-term goals. They give you skills to focus on *right now.* Intermediate goals act as stepping stones to long-term goals. Long-term goals give the entire process purpose and keep you motivated when your enthusiasm lags.

Often, the biggest challenge of goal setting is that although you may have good intentions, following through with all the little details of the process may be challenging. For the program to be successful, you must continually reevaluate your goals. Take time each week to reassess the areas that still need improvement.

> he idea of the Olympics always hung out there in front of me like the carrot in front of the rabbit, but in order to pace myself and avoid getting discouraged by the long process, I set smaller goals for myself along the way.
>
> —*MARY LOU RETTON,[12] 1984 OLYMPIC GOLD MEDALIST, GYMNASTICS*

Visualize your steps to success. Sit down with a pen and reward yourself for your achievements. Set new goals to replace those you have already reached, making sure they are M.A.S.T.E.R. goals. This is important. As Yogi Berra said, "If you don't know where you're going, you could end up someplace else."

Surprisingly, most goal-setting programs go no further than identifying what you would like to accomplish. All the identification in the world makes little difference without *implementation* of the plan. Hopefully, these next exercises can help you plan which goals are most important to you and how to go about meeting and surpassing those goals. As you go through these exercises, take into consideration the criteria for setting M.A.S.T.E.R. goals.

1. *Pick something you wish to achieve. Give it a date of attainment: "I would like to do _____ (action) by _____ (date)."*

2. *Refine this goal to make sure it is a M.A.S.T.E.R. goal (measurable, adaptable, specific, time-bound, encouraging, realistic).*

_____

_____

_____

3. *How will you accomplish this goal? Ask resources like instructors and other golfers about how to answer this question. They should have good suggestions. Be specific! Pay attention to the details necessary for accomplishing this task.*

_____

_____

_____

_____

4. *Identify the obstacles or speed bumps that you could anticipate causing hiccups on your path to peak performance. Again, be specific!*

_____

_____

_____

5. *How will you overcome each of these speed bumps? Identify personal actions here that will help you reach your goal. Highlight and emphasize what you can control in smoothing out these bumps.*

_____

_____

_____

_____

_____

_____

6. *What are the benefits to reaching this goal?*

_____

_____

_____

7. *If you are someone who needs external rewards to maintain motivation, create a contract for yourself here. "If I accomplish _____ (action) by _____ (date), I can _____ (reward)."*

8. *Picture yourself achieving your goal. Imagine the steps it will take to achieve your short-term goals and then eventually your long-term goal. Absorb the feeling of satisfaction and joy. Come back to this image periodically to keep yourself motivated and excited.*

Go through this procedure with the two additional goals that you want to attain this season, which you previously wrote down. Give each of the personal actions you just specified in question 5 dates of attainment. By giving dates of attainment, you should be able to come up with a prioritization of goals. The short-term actions needed to accomplish the goal (question 2) provide you with immediate action. If you hit a snag in attainment, go back to this exercise, and look at your answers to question 5. Remember that your goals need to and can be flexible. If the goal needs to be revised, go ahead and make the necessary adjustments. Your short-term goals should guide you in setting and adjusting intermediate and long-term goals and attainment dates. But don't use the adaptability of goal setting as justification for slacking off. Follow through with your commitment, putting forth the effort needed to reach the goals that will ultimately improve your golf game.

Goal Tree. Another way to visualize your goals is to create a goal tree. Use the following sketch as a guide.

The trunk of the tree is your long-term goal. In this example, it's to lower your handicap from 15 to 10 in two years. Next come the major limbs, on which you may write your intermediate goals. Here the intermediate goals are to play more often, to get fit, to learn key mental training techniques, and to improve your short game. These limb goals become more specific as you branch out to the specific goals, located on the smaller branches. These short-term goals are very specific and plentiful because, as you know, there are many steps to lowering your handicap.

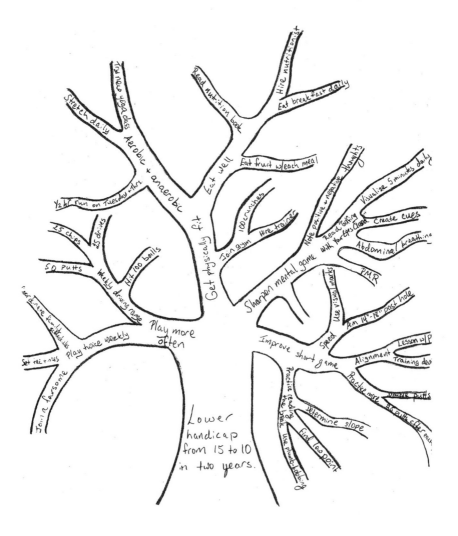

As you create your own goal tree in the provided blank template, feel free to add more branches as you need if you have achieved or adapted a goal on one of the other branches or limbs. You may also want to make copies of this blank goal tree to have additional places to visualize multiple long-term goals.

Imagine that all the branches and limbs provide strength to your tree trunk—the more specific goals you achieve, the closer you come to reaching your end goal in golf. Keep this tree visible, and come up with a system for marking your achievements: perhaps you color in each successful leaf or highlight the ones you are currently practicing. Keeping visual track of your goals helps you achieve them faster. And that means more satisfaction on the links.

Plan of Action

Now take all this information to the calendar! Put your goals into the appropriate dates on your calendar. Break your goals down into what you would like to accomplish each day, in the next week, for the month, and over the entire season. Make up a grading system for goal attainment. At the end of each week, grade how well you attained the week's goals. Give yourself a reward for high scores. The high grades mean you are progressing well through the season.

The most crucial element of the goal-setting process is the weekly goal check. Take a few minutes at the start of each week to review your M.A.S.T.E.R. goals, assess your progress, reward yourself for your achievements, and set new goals once you've reached your old ones. To boost motivation for the next set of challenges, you can visualize the successful feeling you had when accomplishing past goals. Then create mental images of the specific tasks to focus on each day. Use your goal check to make sure you are on track to realizing your long-term goals by completing your short-term goals.

Other Tricks to Help You Stick to Your Goals

→ Share your goals with a teammate or coach, and have them check on your progress each week throughout the season.

→ Introduce this goal-setting program to others with whom you regularly play golf. The more people involved, the easier it is to stick to each task and to hold each other accountable.

→ Write down your long-term goal, and hang it on your wall or put it in your golf bag. Having this constant reminder visible helps you push through the holes when your motivation lags.

→ Occasionally watch movies and read stories of successful golfers; then visualize yourself in their shoes for inspiration and to reinforce your commitment to your goals.

TAKE IT TO THE COURSE!

There may be days when you aren't excited to play or lose your drive partway through a round. Maybe you become less motivated after a few missed shots, a rain delay, or the strain of a competitive foursome. To be a consistent player, you need to be able to revive your motivation at a moment's notice. One of the easiest ways to boost your internal driver is to visualize yourself taking the steps to achieve controllable goals.

So take your list or goal tree with you to the course. Tuck it in your bag where you can reach and read it when you start to drag. Reminding yourself of the goals you are working on keeps you focused on the positive parts of the game and helps you forget the reasons that sent your motivation plummeting. This is why M.A.S.T.E.R. goals are so important. The more measurable, adaptable, specific, time-bound, encouraging, and realistic each goal is, the more driven you will be to step up and go for it. Also, leafing through some of the past goals you set and visualizing the feelings you had after achievement will boost your self-confidence.

SUMMARY

→ Motivation is what fuels your desire to excel in golf.
→ Staying in touch with your intrinsic motivation will carry you further than relying on rewards out of your control.
→ The reasons you give for your golfing success, or lack thereof, influence your motivation on the course.
→ Focus on what you can control in your golf game to enhance motivation.
→ Setting and following through with goals can boost motivation.
→ Setting M.A.S.T.E.R. goals is an effective way you can succeed.
→ Goal setting should include short-, intermediate, and long-term goals.
→ "Ink it, don't just think it!"[13]
→ Visualize your goals to increase your potential to achieve them.
→ Once goals are set, check them weekly to evaluate your progress and to reward your improvement.

Goal setting works, and whether you are aware of it or not, you probably make spontaneous goals for yourself throughout the season. To get the most out of goal setting, start to become aware by taking the time to follow the guidelines for M.A.S.T.E.R. goals. Just by picking up this book, you have demonstrated the desire to improve your game. Take a stance, and commit to actually starting and following through with your personal goal-setting program—go for it! Give yourself the best opportunity for success by visualizing yourself achieving each goal in your tree, from the smallest branch to the central trunk. Be diligent about completing your short-term goals, and pretty soon, your internal driver will put your long-term ambitions within your reach.

HOW FAR HAVE YOU COME?

The questions in this section are designed to assess how far you have come in applying the techniques of this chapter and what you can work on to improve your internal driver. Establish your goal-setting program before completing this section.

1. How have you used imagery to achieve or move closer to your goals?

_____

_____

_____

_____

_____

_____

2. How much time per week have you spent setting, reviewing, and working toward your goals in the last month?

_____

_____

_____

_____

_____

_____

3. In what situations did goal setting help stimulate motivation?

_____

_____

_____

_____

_____

_____

4. Which steps in the goal-setting process did you find most helpful? Make sure to concentrate on these areas as you set goals for future play.

_____

_____

_____

_____

_____

_____

5. For the goals you are still working on, look closely at any obstacles preventing your success. Picture these as "speed bumps" along your path to achievement. What can you do to get over each of these speed bumps and smooth your road to success?

_____

_____

_____

_____

_____

_____

6. Looking back at the question asked about your biggest dream for yourself as a golfer, what are the next steps to take as you progress toward that goal? If there are any additional short-term goals that would help you attain the intermediate goals, take time to write those in your goal journal or as a branch on your goal tree now.

_____

_____

_____

_____

_____

_____

7. Go back and review all the goals you set last month. Which goals were you successful in achieving? Congratulations! Reward yourself for these accomplishments!

_____

_____

_____

THE SIXTH HOLE

Life's Lessons

Many people have compared the game of golf to life. Some of the parallels make sense, and others are just plain silly. Your tee shot certainly isn't going to help when you are faced with a difficult decision in life. Neither will lowering your handicap be of much use to you when you are applying for your next job. However, the mental skills you learn from golf can be translated to life outside the sport.

TEEING OFF

These transferable skills that you have exercised often and have refined can be called on to help you prepare for a presentation, refocus at work or school when you are distracted, control your anxiety when you are in a nervous situation, set goals, and more. At the very beginning of the book, we suggested using imagery to prevent errors, correct mistakes, enhance confidence, assess and perfect skills, calm and energize, encourage healing, and promote success on the course. This chapter takes a look at how visualization can do some of the same things for you in your personal life off the course.

> They say golf is like life, but don't believe them. Golf is more complicated than that.
>
> —GARDNER DICKINSON [1]

One of the things we love most about the mental aspect of all sports is how you can really use it in all areas of life. Explore the areas you find most relevant, and see how you can even improve your "performances" in life.

PICTURE THIS

You may already use visualization in your daily life quite often without realizing it. Have you ever rehearsed in your mind what to say when you call someone on the phone? What about mentally running through a class presentation or meeting briefing? Have you thought through how a job interview might go and how you might respond to the questions asked? Or have you imagined the feeling of stepping out on stage before a musical performance or any other type of performance? Really, anytime you plan how you want to do something and then continue to replay those thoughts in your head, you use imagery.

COACH'S CORNER

Developing players who understand how golf skills can be transferred to life is essential in preparing your athletes for the world outside of golf. As you teach them the mental skills needed to excel in golf, translate the skills to the real world. If they begin to use the techniques both on the course and at home, think how much stronger their mental muscle will be.

We use visualization in our personal lives on a consistent basis. We mentally practice what to say during individual confrontations. We visualize while getting ready for large public-speaking engagements and to prepare for a difficult day ahead. We activate images to overcome writer's block and to picture how an event might unfold. We visualize a driving route in our minds to make sure we know where we're heading. Using visualization helps us be more successful in our jobs and personal lives by instilling the necessary confidence and composure and giving us an active way to prepare for circumstances we face. All in all, mental imagery can help you be prepared in your everyday life so that you may work through challenges effectively.

Self-Assessment Scorecard question 18 addresses your use of visualization in life. Can you think of any activities in daily life where you have used visualization in the past, whether you did it purposely or not?

_____

_____

_____

_____

How do you want to begin using visualization in your everyday life? Be specific.

_____

_____

_____

_____

PLAYER'S POINTER

The next time you're in a big meeting or have to give a presentation, visualize just like you do on the golf course. Take a deep breath, and see yourself preparing to confidently deliver your best performance. Prior to your next interview, visualize yourself dressed for success, giving a firm handshake, answering questions intelligently, and leaving them with a great impression. Visualization is a transferable skill that you can easily use on and off the course.

RELAX!

Has anyone ever told you, "Just relax!" or commented on how stressed out you seem? Maybe you have had the thought, "I can't wait to go on vacation; I really need to relax." In our fast-paced Western culture we place such importance on doing, being, and having that relaxing often gets pushed off or nearly forgotten. Relaxation has become overrated, and overworking and stressed-out living have become the norm. Being loose and relaxed in golf is a must. If you aren't loose, the tension in your muscles causes your body to respond in a way that changes your swing, usually for the worse. The same can be true about life off the course: when you are uptight and not relaxed, your body reacts in ways you do not desire.

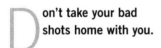

D
on't take your bad
shots home with you.

—*TONY LEMA*[2]

At those moments when you feel stressed out and experience tight muscles, tension headaches, stomachaches, a racing heart, or a rash, perhaps one of the short relaxation techniques described in Chapter 4 can help you. The abdominal breathing techniques are favorites of ours. They are proven to work quickly to calm your mind and heart. You can actually feel the immediate effect that deep breathing can physically have on a racing heart or a tight chest. We know someone who has a note on her phone at work that simply says, "Breathe." This visual cue reminds her to take one deep breath before she picks up the phone, giving her time to focus on and prepare for the call. After all, you never know who is going to be on the other end. It could be an angry client, your boss demanding that report, or your spouse with bad news. Hopefully, that's the rare occasion, but it's best to be prepared and a deep breath can trigger the necessary refocusing.

Another great relaxation technique that hasn't been discussed yet is "Five Minutes in Paradise." What place is paradise for you? Set a timer for five minutes, close your eyes, and picture yourself there. Be sure to make your images vivid, controllable, and positive. You don't need any hurricanes blowing through the beach you are visualizing! While five minutes in paradise may seem like a chunk of time you could otherwise use more productively, just imagine the increased focus you will gain and be able to dedicate to the task after this relaxation exercise.

What do you typically do to relax? Do you truly feel relaxed after this activity?

_____

_____

_____

_____

What relaxation techniques from this book do you want to start practicing in your daily life?

_____

_____

_____

_____

Something else you may try to help relieve stress and reduce anxiety is to picture yourself writing down the things that make you nervous or concerned. For some the physical act of writing is cathartic. If that's you, grab a piece of paper and a pen and actually write those concerns down. Of the things you have written down, either physically on paper or mentally in your mind, ask yourself if there is anything you can do at the present time to make a difference in any of these situations. If the answer is yes, decide how you will act. For those items out of your control at the moment, put them in your mental or physical lockbox. Either visualize yourself dropping these concerns into a solid wooden box and tightly shutting the top, or physically slide your written worries into a real box that you can close. Then either mentally or physically shelve them. You can't do anything about them at the moment, so put them away for later. Release your mind and your body from the stress that comes with holding on to these burdens.

Fretting over things you can't control doesn't usually help, but neither does completely forgetting about them. Return to your lockbox as needed. When you are relaxed, pull out your lockbox of worries to consider if now is the time to act on any of them. If the answer is no, return the box to the shelf and revisit it later. Oftentimes, many of your worries will have dissolved simply by having been put in your lockbox.

FOCUS YOUR ATTENTION

How easy it is to get sidetracked throughout the day. Regardless if you are the CEO of a large company, a university student, a mother of three children, or a bus driver, distractions arise each hour, taking your focus off your job or the tasks you are trying to complete. Just as in golf, triggers are all around. They could include a telephone call, an impromptu meeting, a hungry child, a chatty coworker or classmate, a system error, or a host of other interruptions. Some things we need to give our attention to, like a crying baby or an impromptu meeting, but others we need to find ways to disregard or respond appropriately to, such as the telephone call or chatty coworker. Knowing what interruptions to indulge is the key. As we stated in Chapter 4, focusing on what is in your control is key to regaining proper concentration when you are distracted. You can choose to change the way you are thinking or feeling.

> You are meant to play the ball as it lies, a fact that may help to touch on your own objective approach to life.
>
> —GRANTLAND RICE[3]

What interruptions or distractions do you typically experience each day?

_____

_____

_____

_____

How do you deal with these interruptions that arise?

_____

_____

Set out a plan in advance for handling common distractions. Try using visualization to picture how you will respond the next time. Whether you want to consider the polite way to advise your coworker that you need to focus on what you're doing at the moment, or choose to respond to your screaming child with patience, or decide not answer the phone if you are not in a good frame of mind or location to talk, you can prepare yourself for any scenario. With time and practice, your mind and your body will respond the way you have trained them in your imagery sessions.

ON THE STAGE OF LIFE

If you think about it, life is a performance of sorts. Outside of the four walls of your home, that performance becomes a bit more obvious. At work or school, with friends or strangers, you may feel even more on stage. Being confident of what you do and who you are can take you a great distance both personally and professionally. It's amazing the difference just imagining yourself feeling and looking confident can make for you. Before your next important event, take a few minutes to see yourself appearing confident—head up, shoulders back, face calm—and sense the feeling of confidence in your body.

Do you remember what the key to confidence was in Chapter 3? The answer is consistent positive thinking. This can be a challenging thing to try to achieve in your golf game, much less your life. If you are naturally an optimist person, this may come fairly easily. For the "glass half empty" folks, this is a greater hurdle to cross.

Do you remember the thinking, feeling, performing cycle we discussed earlier? If you are confident, you are more likely to think positively and to set challenging goals. You are also more likely to exert the time and energy needed to achieve your goals. When goals are achieved, your confidence increases and there's a greater chance you can put out the effort needed to set and reach a new goal. Seems pretty simple, but it must start with what you can control: how you are thinking.

So what are you thinking? What negative thoughts about yourself do you tend to have? In what areas do you doubt yourself or put yourself down? Start attacking this negative self-talk by using the methods discussed in Chapter 3. You will find they work just as well with personal self-talk as they do with golf self-talk.

Who is the most confident person you admire? What qualities can you try to emulate?

_____

_____

_____

_____

In your life, for what "performances" do you need confidence?

_____

_____

_____

_____

In what areas of life do you find yourself having the most negative self-talk?

_____

_____

_____

_____

IN THE COURSE OF LIFE

Bill

From the age of seven through to my summers at caddy camp, my clubs were old hand-me-downs—I even continued to play with my favorite wooden-shafted blade putter after cracking and taping it up. Several years later, my uncle gave me his old steel-shafted woods. The spoon was so versatile—I used that club with great success.

One afternoon, playing with my uncle, my tee shot rolled to a stop on the downhill side of the fairway. The green was a long spoon shot away. So I took out my trusty 3-wood, stepped up to the ball, adjusted my stance to the downhill lie, and swung away. I topped the shot, and the ball dribbled down the hill and into the rough. Disgusted and angry, I raised the club over my head and flung it after the ball. With a sickening metallic ping, the shaft broke into two pieces. My favorite 3-wood—gone! My anger evaporated instantly. Chagrin took over.

It was the last time I lost my temper playing golf—or any other sport. In fact, keeping my cool in tense situations has proven invaluable throughout my life: in college, with my family, and in my own businesses with multiple employees and facilities.

As a husband, I hug my wife frequently and tell her I love her every day. As a father, I try to instill confidence in my kids and encourage them to go for their dreams. As a business owner, I worked hard to make sure my customers were happy.

Every day, when I wake up and look out at the view from our kitchen window, I feel lucky to be in good health, surrounded by a loving family. Whenever something positive happens—a beautiful sunshiny day, a family gathering for a special occasion, or my son-in-law mowing my lawn—no matter how small the blessing, I say, "I'm a lucky daw-w-g!" This has become a family phrase because I say it so often. And I say it because I really feel lucky every day. It's just an optimistic outlook. I always do look at the bright side and because of that outlook, I always feel that, "I'm a lucky daw-w-g."

Author's note: Bill is the most optimistic person I know . . . and he's also my father. As my dad, he makes me feel confident and loved, and positive about life. He is also the one who first taught me to visualize my sport performance, back when I was seven years old.—T.W.

M.A.S.T.E.R. YOUR FUTURE

If you are like us, life can run away with you pretty quickly. Where did that week go? Where did that year go? I can't believe I'm thirty . . . forty . . . fifty. It seems like just yesterday when . . . . Many of our conversations revolve around time and our disbelief at its passing. Setting and pursuing goals is an excellent way both to determine how you want to wisely use the years you have ahead of you and to make a mark on this world.

How will you use your life? What do you want to accomplish? What do you want to experience? How do you want to live? What changes do you want to make to the way you currently live your life? Where do you want to be in six months, five years, ten years?

Use the same steps from Chapter 5 to create your personal goals:

1. *Pick something you wish to achieve. Give it a date of attainment: "I would like to do _____ (action) by _____ (date)."*

2. *Refine this goal to make sure it is a M.A.S.T.E.R. goal (measurable, adaptable, specific, time-bound, encouraging, realistic).*

_____

_____

_____

3. *How will you accomplish this goal? Ask resources like family and colleagues about how to answer this question. They should have good suggestions. Be specific! Pay attention to the details necessary for accomplishing this task.*

_____

_____

_____

_____

4. *Identify the obstacles, or speed bumps, that you could anticipate causing hiccups on your path to peak performance. Again, be specific!*

_____

_____

_____

_____

5. *How will you overcome each of these speed bumps? Identify personal actions here that will help you reach your goal. Highlight and emphasize what you can control in smoothing out these bumps.*

_____

_____

_____

_____

_____

6. *What are the benefits to reaching this goal?*

_____

_____

_____

7. *If you are someone who needs external rewards to maintain motivation, create a contract for yourself here. "If I accomplish _____ (action) by _____ (date), I can _____ (reward)."*

8. *Picture yourself achieving your goal. Imagine the steps it will take to achieve your short-term goals and then eventually your long-term goal. Absorb the feeling of satisfaction and joy. Come back to this image periodically to keep yourself motivated and excited.*

Go through this procedure every time you set a goal. Remember that your goals need to and can be flexible. If the goal needs to be revised, go ahead and make the necessary adjustments. Your short-term goals should guide you in setting and adjusting intermediate and long-term goals and attainment dates. But don't use the adaptability of goal setting as justification for slacking off. Follow through with your commitment, putting forth the effort needed to reach the goals, which will enhance your life.

TAKE IT TO THE COURSE OF LIFE

There is much to be gleaned from the mental side of golf. It's exciting to know that following the exercises in this book will benefit you on the course and if you choose, off the course in your personal life, too. This is only scratching the surface. As you play the game, consider other ways the physical and mental components of this great sport complement and carry over to your life.

What other lessons have you learned from the game of golf?

_____

_____

_____

Using these visualization techniques both on and off the course will contribute to your strength in each aspect of your life.

Sample Golf
Visualization Scripts

Y ou've now reached the golden key to the whole shebang. This section has visualization templates for many different situations you will meet on the course. We've crafted each script to give you an idea of some of the sights, sounds, and feelings you may want to mentally rehearse on a regular basis. The scripts should be used as springboards to help you create your own visualization routines. To get going, use ours; then individualize your own with personal skills, rituals and routines, areas of improvement, and so on. Everyone's images will be different, but these scripts provide you with a jumping-off point.

Right before you play, you may find you have little time or are cramped for space to lie down and relax. That's OK: imagery is a skill you can perform anywhere, anytime. All you need to do is narrow your focus, mentally block out any distractions, and go to that familiar, confident scene in your mind. You can visualize quickly and effectively without anyone even noticing. Even a few seconds of mental rehearsal—perhaps just as you walk up to the tee box, as part of your pre-shot routine, or between shots—helps you prepare to compete.

As we have reiterated throughout this book, be patient with yourself as you implement imagery into your game. Follow the initial timetables discussed in Chapter 2, and begin using the imagery scripts included in this chapter and the ones you create for yourself as you become ready.

The steps to using the guided mental imagery scripts are threefold. First, begin by relaxing. Follow the brief relaxation exercise, using your body to prepare your mind for a visualizing session. Next, take a few minutes to read through the script before you try actively imaging. It should trigger within you the excitement you feel on the course. You may want to reread the script a few times to familiarize yourself with the scene. Once you have the general gist, visualize the scene yourself and let your imagination fill in the details. After you have played through the scenario, consider the "Mix It Up" variations. Try out a few of the possible changes, or simply replay the original script on a different course. Finally, after you have rehearsed a few times, review the "O.P.E.N. Your Mind" reminders to ensure you are including the important elements of visualization.

We even recommend you make an audio recording of the script (or of a script you subsequently create—see Chapter 8, "Design Your Own Visualization Scripts"). Then you can relax, listen to the script, and be guided through your mental rehearsal without the distraction of reading along. Consider these personal visualization scripts to be a set of keys, all of which open different doors to peak performance. The more keys you have, the more chances you have of opening the doors consistently.

Put all the keys in the right locks at the right time, and you'll achieve your dreams.

Pretournament Warm-Up

This script is designed to be used as you prepare to play under pressure. The warm-up is a time when imagery is easy to incorporate and very effective in reducing tension.

Start by Relaxing

To begin, find a comfortable place to sit or lie down, and close your eyes. Take three deep abdominal breaths, exhaling slowly each time. As you exhale, imagine that tension throughout your body begins to flow away. Starting at your toes and working your way up to the top of your head, mentally scan your body for areas of tension. As you discover tension, contract the muscles in that area for ten seconds, then relax for fifteen seconds, and then contract for another ten seconds, followed by fifteen seconds of relaxation. Go through this contracting and relaxing cycle one more time. Continue scanning, looking for areas that need to be relaxed. Once you reach the top of your head, scan back down to your toes, noting any areas you may have missed. When you arrive back at your toes, take three more deep abdominal breaths. You are ready to visualize.

Visualize

You arrive at the course with the sounds of your favorite music filling the car. You are relaxed and feeling good about the day ahead. Having arrived at the course about an hour and a half before your tee time, you know you have plenty of time to warm up and get yourself both physically and mentally prepared for the round. You get out of the car, deeply inhale the morning air, and unload your clubs. Check the pockets of your bag to make sure you have all the right gear for the day. You change into your golf shoes, grab your lucky hat, and make your way to the starters' table.

Check in at the starters' table, and confirm your tee time. Things are running on time. You proceed to the range to begin warming up, noticing other competitors as you walk, all going through their own warm-up routine. A nervous quietness is in the air. You say, "Hi," and smile at a few who make eye contact with you, and then you locate an open spot to hit.

You begin with a few basic stretches, breathing deeply, working out any nervousness, and focusing your mind on this moment and your routine. Repeat your mental mantra to yourself as you loosen up your arms, neck, back, and shoulders. You are ready and excited to start hitting.

Take out a wedge, and start by hitting a few shots to a target. Stretch a bit more before you pull your 8-iron out from your bag. As you hit some full shots with your iron, you feel good and fluid as you swing through the ball. You react to the target—thanks to your hard practice, your body is responding without your mind getting in the way.

The person next to you starts hitting drives, but you stay focused on your routine, working your way through your bag from more lofted clubs to less lofted clubs. You stay relaxed, continuing to breathe deeply, and repeat your mantra as you enjoy a quiet peace with yourself. A range person drops off some balls for you. You say, "Thanks," and keep going. You are finding and settling into your rhythm for the day.

You take off the head cover of one of your fairway woods and hit a few woods. Next, you pull out your driver, reach into your bag to get some tees, and place them in your pocket. One by one, you tee up some balls to hit with your driver. You pick your target and go, remembering your swing thought as you rip it. Tee up again and hit the ball, staying balanced as you swing hard through. You maintain your tempo, without being distracted by others around you, and stay within your own swing. You're feeling good and ready to practice chipping.

You walk over to the chipping area and put down a few balls. Before each chip, you visualize yourself putting the ball in the hole. You know if you focus and see the ball going into the hole on every chip shot, you will have a chance to make it. Again, you let your body react to the target, not forcing or overthinking a shot. Chip some shots to shorter targets, using your various wedges.

Feeling good about your short game, you throw a few balls into the practice bunker and hit a few shots out. You want to make sure you get a feel for the sand before you are out on the course. You finish hitting out of the sand and rake the bunker before you move on to the practice green.

As you continue to the practice green, keep preparing yourself physically by taking a few drinks from your water bottle, as well as mentally by breathing deeply and repeating your mantra to yourself. Enjoy the striking sound of club-faces contacting balls and the smell of the grass as you walk.

Go through your drills on the practice green, making sure to remove one of the flags to give yourself a setting similar to that on the actual course. As you putt, imagine different situations you might encounter on the course. You know placing this pressure on yourself now will help you perform better when you actually face the situation. You are thankful your coach made you do this in practice. You've seen it pay off and know it is one more way you can help your body respond to a situation without your mind getting in the way.

You check your watch—you have just enough time to make a stop at the restroom before heading to the first tee. When you return, the speaker announces your name as being "on deck," so you move toward the first tee. You meet the other players in your group and go through the standard procedures of exchanging cards with everyone and showing your ball.

Pull out your driver and take a few swings. You place an extra tee in your pocket and make sure you have a ball marker. Your name is announced. You walk up to the tee, and your pre-shot routine begins. Tee up your ball and breathe deeply as you proceed through your routine, staying in your rhythm. Your thoughts are focused on this moment, and you are ready to send the ball. You rip your shot down the fairway, and you are off to a good start!

Mix It Up. Try different variations of this script. Can you see yourself at different courses? How does changing the weather affect the routine? What if it's rainy or cold? Try doing this routine in a different order, perhaps beginning on the putting green. You may want to try visualizing specific holes you are challenged by and work on making those difficult shots. Put yourself in the position of winning the tournament with the next shot or moving into the lead. How do you handle the pressure? What are the important elements of your performance? Make sure you are including these elements as you go through your performance in your mind.

O.P.E.N. Your Mind. Remember this feeling, this confidence, this satisfaction. Replay this routine in your head as part of your training regimen. See and feel every element of the different parts of a hole. Tune into the sounds, smells, and even tastes of performance. The more details you can visualize, the better your body can prepare.

As you're learning and perfecting your technique, use the following tips to O.P.E.N. yourself to improvement.

→ **Observe:** Did you visualize *internally* or *externally*? Some of both? What was most helpful from each view?

→ **Positive Practice:** If any negative images squeezed in, take a moment now to rewind your mental video, slow it down, and replace each mistake with a *positive* image. Repeat a cue word or action—maybe your mental mantra—to trigger this positive image. Replay the positive replacement at least three times to make sure it sticks in your mind.

→ **Experiment:** Can you mentally *slow down* your stroke speed and analyze your technique? Can you change the tempo of your swing? This is *control*. It takes practice! Often, slowing down your images and playing your "mental movie" frame by frame allows you to control your performance in your mind.

→ **Notice:** Could you actually *feel* your body's movements, even slightly? This is the goal of guided imagery. Tune into the sounds, smells, and even tastes of performance. The more details you can visualize, the better your body can prepare. Visualizing yourself staying composed, focused on the present moment, and able to move on to the next shot is a great way to prepare for the unexpected.

Teeing Off

This script is designed to help you manage your nerves and pre-shot routine. Visualizing yourself teeing off is one of the fundamental skills of mastering golf imagery.

Start by Relaxing

To begin, find a comfortable place to sit or lie down, and close your eyes. Take three deep abdominal breaths, exhaling slowly each time. As you exhale, imagine that tension throughout your body begins to flow away. Starting at your toes and working your way up to the top of your head, mentally scan your body for areas of tension. As you discover tension, contract the muscles in that area for ten seconds, then relax for fifteen seconds, and then contract for another ten seconds, followed by fifteen seconds of relaxation. Go through this contracting and relaxing cycle one more time. Continue scanning, looking for areas that need to be relaxed. Once you reach the top of your head, scan back down to your toes, noting any areas you may have missed. When you arrive back at your toes, take three more deep abdominal breaths. You are ready to visualize.

Visualize

It is a chilly, drizzly morning. You are playing with a new group today, having met only one of them before. The other two are business partners of your friend, and you want to look like you know what you're doing. This is your home course, so you feel you know it well.

You are first off, so go to your bag to choose your club for this 340-yard par-four. In your mind, you are debating about using your driver, but you are not completely confident of your accuracy with it. You feel more comfortable with your 5-wood, but you don't want anyone to think you can't handle your driver. You can feel the other players watching you, and it makes you nervous.

Your hands are damp as they encircle your 5-wood. You've decided to use the club you can trust. Pulling it out of your bag, you unzip the pocket and grab a ball and tee; then you quickly walk over and tee up your ball. This hole bends to the right around a dogleg, has a water hazard on the right about 200 yards down, tall oak trees lining the left side of the fairway, and two bunkers on the front and back of the green. The hole is right behind the front bunker.

As you plan your game, you visualize each shot of this hole in your mind. You will first hit a controlled fade to the middle of the fairway. From there, you should be able to lay up, then chip a gentle approach shot onto the green, and putt in for four. With your plan set, you focus intently on the first shot.

Performing your pre-shot routine includes using your cues to trigger positive images of your relaxed grip and powerful swing. You say to yourself, "I can do it!" inhale deeply, and take your practice swing. Once more you look at your target; then you address the ball. As you plant your feet and aim your toe line a little left of your target, repeat your swing thought—your mental mantra: "I can do it!" and release your body. Take a deep, calming breath, and feel your whole body—arms, back, trunk, head, and legs—coordinate in a beautiful, compact, outside-in swing. You hear the perfect sound of contact and watch the ball's sidespin bend it right at your target. You're off! You're picking up your tee as your friend pats you on the back to congratulate you for a terrific first shot.

Mix It Up. Visualize a similar scene on a different hole. What does it look like? Where is your target? Can you create a change in the weather in your mental movie? How does the pressure change if you're teeing off with a group of good friends or in your club tournament? Visualize performing your favorite techniques for regulating your nerves. Every time you tee off, see and feel yourself in each tee box concentrating on the drive you are about to hit. Mentally zoom in to the present moment, blocking out any past shots (good or bad), distractions, and sources of pressure. Remind yourself of the key triggers: perhaps your grip, your practice swing, your foot placement, your deep breath. What clubs will you use as you make your way from the tee, to the fairway, to the green, and into the hole?

O.P.E.N. Your Mind. Remember this feeling, this confidence, this satisfaction. Replay this routine in your head as part of your training regimen. See and feel every element of the different parts of a hole. Tune into the sounds, smells, and even tastes of performance. The more details you can visualize, the better your body can prepare.

As you're learning and perfecting your technique, use the following tips to O.P.E.N. yourself to improvement.

→ **Observe:** Did you visualize *internally* or *externally*? Some of both? What was most helpful from each view?
→ **Positive Practice:** If any negative images squeezed in, take a moment now to rewind your mental video, slow it down, and replace each mistake with a *positive* image. Repeat a cue word or action—maybe your mental mantra—to trigger this positive image. Replay the positive replacement at least three times to make sure it sticks in your mind.

→ **Experiment:** Can you mentally *slow down* your stroke speed and analyze your technique? Can you change the tempo of your swing? This is *control*. It takes practice! Often, slowing down your images and playing your "mental movie" frame by frame allows you to control your performance in your mind.

→ **Notice:** Could you actually *feel* your body's movements, even slightly? This is the goal of guided imagery. Tune into the sounds, smells, and even tastes of performance. The more details you can visualize, the better your body can prepare. Visualizing yourself staying composed, focused on the present moment, and able to move on to the next shot is a great way to prepare for the unexpected.

Playing from the Rough

It's always a challenge, both physically and mentally, to hit a good shot from the rough. This script leads you through the thoughts and triggers that can help you get back in the game.

Start by Relaxing

To begin, find a comfortable place to sit or lie down, and close your eyes. Take three deep abdominal breaths, exhaling slowly each time. As you exhale, imagine that tension throughout your body begins to flow away. Starting at your toes and working your way up to the top of your head, mentally scan your body for areas of tension. As you discover tension, contract the muscles in that area for ten seconds, then relax for fifteen seconds, and then contract for another ten seconds, followed by fifteen seconds of relaxation. Go through this contracting and relaxing cycle one more time. Continue scanning, looking for areas that need to be relaxed. Once you reach the top of your head, scan back down to your toes, noting any areas you may have missed. When you arrive back at your toes, take three more deep abdominal breaths. You are ready to visualize.

Visualize

On your drive, you got distracted at the last minute, thinking about too many aspects of your swing mechanics: keeping your head still, aiming the back of your left hand at the target, positioning your clubhead, loosening your grip, keeping your weight on your forward foot, and even second-guessing your club choice. Now you find yourself on a pretty steep upslope deep in the rough.

You've been in a similar situation before and were able to successfully get back in the game. But you're concerned that you might not be as lucky this time.

And people are watching, making you feel even less confident. In your mind, replay the satisfied feeling you had the last time you got out of the rough on a slope like this. Remember to take your time, be patient, and stick to your prep routine.

Now choose your club. Remember, as challenging as it may be to pick the right one, it's your commitment to your choice that really matters. Recall Rocco Mediate's firm, quick decision on the seventy-second hole of the final round of the 2008 U.S. Open: "What's the total again?" he asked his caddy. And before the caddy could even finish saying, "246," Rocco decided, "This is an 8-iron," and eagerly grabbed the club from his own bag. Make the decision, and then move on to making the shot, leaving the other club choices behind (mentally and physically).

Next, as part of your pre-shot routine, visualize the shot you want to make. Perhaps you have decided to lay up to save par. See and feel yourself playing the ball off your right foot and feel the clubhead behind your hands at contact. Watch yourself holding your shoulders parallel to the slope, staying level with the lie. See the ball launching off the slope and advancing up the fairway. Give yourself a couple of practice swings, duplicating the motions you just rehearsed in your head.

As you prepare to the address the ball, focus your eyes on your target, settle your feet, and feel your grip. Take a deep breath, repeat your swing thought or mental mantra—and go. Thwack! You hear the sound of solid contact and watch the ball fly onto the fairway. You're back in the game!

Mix It Up. Visualize yourself in similar challenging situations so you can prepare to handle them with composure. See your ball sitting down in a bunker, ten yards to the green. Or imagine that you've hit a banana ball and now find yourself so close to a tree trunk that you barely have room for your backswing. Or visualize a situation where you have shanked it out of bounds. How do you handle the pressure created by these adverse conditions? What techniques do you use to keep yourself positive and to block out the negative thoughts of your plugged lie or one stroke penalty?

O.P.E.N. Your Mind. Remember this feeling, this confidence, this satisfaction. Replay this routine in your head as part of your training regimen. See and feel every element of the different parts of a hole. Tune into the sounds, smells, and even tastes of performance. The more details you can visualize, the better your body can prepare.

As you're learning and perfecting your technique, use the following tips to O.P.E.N. yourself to improvement.

→ **Observe:** Did you visualize *internally* or *externally*? Some of both? What was most helpful from each view?

→ **Positive Practice:** If any negative images squeezed in, take a moment now to rewind your mental video, slow it down, and replace each mistake with a *positive* image. Repeat a cue word or action—maybe your mental mantra—to trigger this positive image. Replay the positive replacement at least three times to make sure it sticks in your mind.

→ **Experiment:** Can you mentally *slow down* your stroke speed and analyze your technique? Can you change the tempo of your swing? This is *control*. It takes practice! Often, slowing down your images and playing your "mental movie" frame by frame allows you to control your performance in your mind.

→ **Notice:** Could you actually *feel* your body's movements, even slightly? This is the goal of guided imagery. Tune into the sounds, smells, and even tastes of performance. The more details you can visualize, the better your body can prepare. Visualizing yourself staying composed, focused on the present moment, and able to move on to the next shot is a great way to prepare for the unexpected.

Recovering from a Poor Shot

You've probably been in a situation where you had to scramble to regain composure after a lousy shot. This script is designed to help you mentally rehearse what it takes to recover and to physically and emotionally move on to the next shot.

Start by Relaxing

To begin, find a comfortable place to sit or lie down, and close your eyes. Take three deep abdominal breaths, exhaling slowly each time. As you exhale, imagine that tension throughout your body begins to flow away. Starting at your toes and working your way up to the top of your head, mentally scan your body for areas of tension. As you discover tension, contract the muscles in that area for ten seconds, then relax for fifteen seconds, and then contract for another ten seconds, followed by fifteen seconds of relaxation. Go through this contracting and relaxing cycle one more time. Continue scanning, looking for areas that need to be relaxed. Once you reach the top of your head, scan back down to your toes, noting any areas you may have missed. When you arrive back at your toes, take three more deep abdominal breaths. You are ready to visualize.

Visualize

You've really gotten yourself into a pickle this time. One wild shot and you're totally off your game. Your concentration is gone. You've started to think about the score you could have had, why that last shot went awry, the easy putt you missed back on thirteen, how you're going to try to save par, and even why you decided to play today in the first place. Your mind is scrambling to focus, and you feel your muscle tension growing. It is essential that you refocus to get yourself under control, but you aren't even sure where to start.

Remember to quickly go through the stages fudge, fix, forget, and focus. First, release your frustration in a controlled way. Next, visualize what you would have done to fix that technical error: perhaps you would change your stance, your backswing, or the angle of your clubface. Then forget your error with a positive replacement image and a deep breath.

The final step to gathering your composure is to focus one at a time on the things you can control: your breathing and other relaxation techniques, your club choice, your pre-shot routine, how you will address the ball, and your target. Take a couple of deep, calming breaths. Breathe in confidence, breathe out nerves, breathe in peace, breathe out anxiety. These breaths help you calm down and block out the distracting, damaging thoughts about the uncontrollables.

Go through an abbreviated PMR, starting with your head and neck, and moving through your shoulders, arms, back, and legs. Squeeze each muscle group for a few seconds, then relax, and let the frustration melt away.

Do not choose your club until you feel calm and in control. If you need to, use a calming breath as you reach in your bag, and imagine you are pulling out a staff of confidence. This is your time to reinflate your confidence by boldly choosing and committing to your club.

With this confidence, begin your pre-shot routine. In your routine, you first put on your glove, fastening it tightly around the back of your hand. Look at your target in the distance, and repeat your mental mantra: "I'm coming to get you!" This positive thought helps you forget about the previous shot by driving your energy toward the present.

You address the ball with certainty. You know you are going to make it.

Mix It Up. The easiest way to prepare for all kinds of mistakes, lapses of concentration, poor conditions, and pressure shots is by visualizing yourself recovering strongly. Practice seeing, hearing, feeling, and even smelling and tasting yourself coming back after a devastating front nine. How would you turn your day around? What could you do to get yourself back on track? What might you say to yourself? How much of your frustration depends on the things you can control—your swing, your concentration, your experience—and how much depends on the uncontrollables—others' opinions, the course conditions, the score? Focus on the controllables, and you will feel more confident and composed.

O.P.E.N. Your Mind. Remember this feeling, this confidence, this satisfaction. Replay this routine in your head as part of your training regimen. See and feel every element of the different parts of a hole. Tune into the sounds, smells, and even tastes of performance. The more details you can visualize, the better your body can prepare.

As you're learning and perfecting your technique, use the following tips to O.P.E.N. yourself to improvement.

→ **Observe:** Did you visualize *internally* or *externally*? Some of both? What was most helpful from each view?

→ **Positive Practice:** If any negative images squeezed in, take a moment now to rewind your mental video, slow it down, and replace each mistake with a *positive* image. Repeat a cue word or action—maybe your mental mantra—to trigger this positive image. Replay the positive replacement at least three times to make sure it sticks in your mind.

→ **Experiment:** Can you mentally *slow down* your stroke speed and analyze your technique? Can you change the tempo of your swing? This is *control.* It takes practice! Often, slowing down your images and playing your "mental movie" frame by frame allows you to control your performance in your mind.

→ **Notice:** Could you actually *feel* your body's movements, even slightly? This is the goal of guided imagery. Tune into the sounds, smells, and even tastes of performance. The more details you can visualize, the better your body can prepare. Visualizing yourself staying composed, focused on the present moment, and able to move on to the next shot is a great way to prepare for the unexpected.

Putting for Par

Mentally committing to a shot is a tough task. This script helps you block out the thoughts of your potential score and focus instead on exactly what is necessary to make the shot at hand.

Start by Relaxing

To begin, find a comfortable place to sit or lie down, and close your eyes. Take three deep abdominal breaths, exhaling slowly each time. As you exhale, imagine that tension throughout your body begins to flow away. Starting at your toes and working your way up to the top of your head, mentally scan your body for areas of tension. As you discover tension, contract the muscles in that area for ten seconds, then relax for fifteen seconds, and then contract for another ten seconds, followed by fifteen seconds of relaxation. Go through this contracting and relaxing cycle one more time. Continue scanning, looking for areas that need to be relaxed. Once you reach the top of your head, scan back down to your toes, noting any areas you may have missed. When you arrive back at your toes, take three more deep abdominal breaths. You are ready to visualize.

Visualize

Walking up the fairway to your third shot, you see that you are on the green with an eight-foot putt for par. Take your putter from your bag and walk over behind the ball. Squat down and read your putt from behind the ball; then stand up and walk to the other side where you can see the ball on the far side of the hole. You can see that it breaks left uphill and that you need decent speed. If it's not played strongly enough, the ball will move a good bit to the left. You know you must match your speed with the break. Visualize exactly where you will aim: eight inches outside right. Read your putt one more time to be sure your plan is going to work. Take the time to be 100 percent committed to the read. Then, and only then, stand up and walk over to your ball.

You are feeling energized because you *know* you are going to drain it. Begin your pre-shot routine and visualize yourself going through your physical movement, deep breath, and mental mantra. Take one or two practice strokes, imprinting the correct feeling on your brain and muscle memory. As you take these practice strokes, visualize the ball following that exact line off your clubface and into the hole.

Inch forward with your feet so that you are close enough to hit the ball. Ground the club and plant your feet. Feel your spikes gripping firmly into the green, giving you a solid base. You are almost ready. Look at the hole one more time; then narrow your focus to include only the ball and your club. Repeat your mental mantra and go.

Mix It Up. It's likely that you've been distracted when putting. Perhaps you second-guess your read or can't forget your last shot, or maybe someone makes a noise. Whenever an irrelevant thought comes to mind, back off. From this position, you may go through the mental techniques that help you refocus, such as picture-perfect image replacement, positive thinking, or deep breathing. Only when you have completely eliminated all distractions should you address the ball again. Once your mind is clear, restart your prep routine, move into your practice strokes, inch forward, place your clubhead behind the ball, settle your feet, repeat your mental mantra, and go. This whole process need only take a few seconds. But those few seconds can mean the difference between lipping out and sinking it.

O.P.E.N. Your Mind. Remember this feeling, this confidence, this satisfaction. Replay this routine in your head as part of your training regimen. See and feel every element of the different parts of a hole. Tune into the sounds, smells, and even tastes of performance. The more details you can visualize, the better your body can prepare.

As you're learning and perfecting your technique, use the following tips to O.P.E.N. yourself to improvement.

→ **Observe:** Did you visualize *internally* or *externally?* Some of both? What was most helpful from each view?

→ **Positive Practice:** If any negative images squeezed in, take a moment now to rewind your mental video, slow it down, and replace each mistake with a *positive* image. Repeat a cue word or action—maybe your mental mantra—to trigger this positive image. Replay the positive replacement at least three times to make sure it sticks in your mind.

→ **Experiment:** Can you mentally *slow down* your stroke speed and analyze your technique? Can you change the tempo of your swing? This is *control.* It takes practice! Often, slowing down your images and playing your "mental movie" frame by frame allows you to control your performance in your mind.

→ **Notice:** Could you actually *feel* your body's movements, even slightly? This is the goal of guided imagery. Tune into the sounds, smells, and even tastes of performance. The more details you can visualize, the better your body can prepare. Visualizing yourself staying composed, focused on the present moment, and able to move on to the next shot is a great way to prepare for the unexpected.

Putting for Bogey (or Worse)

It happens to even the best players. You know that even if you make this shot, your score will still be higher than you'd hoped. The script will guide you to push through and concentrate on the present moment, regardless of the impending disappointment.

Start by Relaxing

To begin, find a comfortable place to sit or lie down, and close your eyes. Take three deep abdominal breaths, exhaling slowly each time. As you exhale, imagine that tension throughout your body begins to flow away. Starting at your toes and working your way up to the top of your head, mentally scan your body for areas of tension. As you discover tension, contract the muscles in that area for ten seconds, then relax for fifteen seconds, and then contract for another ten seconds, followed by fifteen seconds of relaxation. Go through this contracting and relaxing cycle one more time. Continue scanning, looking for areas that need to be relaxed. Once you reach the top of your head, scan back down to your toes, noting any areas you may have missed. When you arrive back at your toes, take three more deep abdominal breaths. You are ready to visualize.

Visualize

This par-four hole started off badly and hasn't improved. You've finally made it to the green, but it took you three shots to get here. Then you misread the break of the first putt and left the ball five feet from the hole. You are frustrated. You know if you don't take time to focus in right now and gut this putt, you could end up with a double bogey.

Nerves settle into your stomach. You really want to sink the putt and are feeling the pressure you are placing on yourself. Remember to take a few deep breaths to help calm your nervous energy and repeat your mental mantra to yourself. Your mind is racing with thoughts about the last four shots and how poorly you have played up to this point. Use a positive replacement to wipe out the negative thoughts that have the potential of bringing you down. Accept what has happened up to this point, knowing there is no rewind button to push. What's been done is done. All you control at this moment is how you will respond to the putt ahead of you. Take another deep breath, and picture yourself confident and ready. Visualize yourself nailing this putt.

Walk around behind the ball, and get a read on the green. You effectively block out all noise and focus in, not being distracted by anything around you. It's a short putt and you don't want to overthink it, but you still need to play smart. You have a clean and clear line to the hole. The greens have been playing fast today, and you take that into consideration as you mentally prepare for your shot. Feeling good about your read, address the ball and go through your pre-shot routine. You are confident. You know this ball is going in. Together your arms and putter swing smoothly like a pendulum and solidly hit the ball.

Mix It Up. Try different variations of this script. How does this hole end? Did you sink the putt? Try playing this hole from the beginning. Consider what you did to get yourself in this position and how might you have done things differently. Put yourself in different situations—are you putting at the state championship or at a local tournament? Maybe you are just playing a round with friends. How does the pressure change in each situation? When pressure increases, how do you respond? Does your focus get too narrow and cause you to forget about all the relevant triggers? What techniques can you use to help you regulate your mental energy level?

O.P.E.N. Your Mind. Remember this feeling, this confidence, this satisfaction. Replay this routine in your head as part of your training regimen. See and feel every element of the different parts of a hole. Tune into the sounds, smells, and even tastes of performance. The more details you can visualize, the better your body can prepare.

As you're learning and perfecting your technique, use the following tips to O.P.E.N. yourself to improvement.

→ **Observe:** Did you visualize *internally* or *externally*? Some of both?
→ **Positive Practice:** If any negative images squeezed in, take a moment now to rewind your mental video and replace them with *positive* images. Repeat a cue word or action—maybe your mental mantra—to trigger this positive image. Replay the positive replacement at least three times to make sure it sticks in your mind.
→ **Experiment:** Can you *slow down* your stroke speed and analyze your technique? Can you change the tempo of your swing? This is *control*. It takes practice! Often, slowing down your images and playing your "mental movie" frame by frame allows you to control your performance in your mind.
→ **Notice:** Could you actually *feel* your body's movements, even slightly? This is the goal of guided imagery. Tune into the sounds, smells, and even tastes of performance. The more details you can visualize, the better your body can prepare. Visualizing yourself staying composed, focused on the present moment, and able to move on to the next shot is a great way to prepare for the unexpected.

Breaking 100-90-80

Whatever the score you're aiming to break, you'll experience extra pressure as you approach your goal. This script is designed to help you manage that pressure so that you will be able to make the shots you need to get the score you want.

Start by Relaxing
To begin, find a comfortable place to sit or lie down, and close your eyes. Take three deep abdominal breaths, exhaling slowly each time. As you exhale, imagine that tension throughout your body begins to flow away. Starting at your toes and working your way up to the top of your head, mentally scan your body for areas of tension. As you discover tension, contract the muscles in that area for ten seconds, then relax for fifteen seconds, and then contract for another ten seconds, followed by fifteen seconds of relaxation. Go through this contracting and

relaxing cycle one more time. Continue scanning, looking for areas that need to be relaxed. Once you reach the top of your head, scan back down to your toes, noting any areas you may have missed. When you arrive back at your toes, take three more deep abdominal breaths. You are ready to visualize.

Visualize

You have been working toward your goal of breaking 90 the past few months, getting closer with each round and each tournament played. There have been a few times you came so close, but let the excitement and nervous energy of reaching your goal take over. Today you are making another run at it. You shot a 44 on the front nine and have played a solid back nine so far. You're walking off the seventeenth hole, having just made par. Tallying your score, you notice you are shooting a 40 for the back nine and you are feeling really good. Just one hole remains to be played in the round. "Bring it on," you think to yourself, "All I have to do is par this next hole and I'll be at 88!"

Take one step back. This is exactly the unintended pressure you have placed on yourself every time you have been this close in the past. Give yourself a mental time-out and focus on the present. Wipe the picture from your mind of making your putt for par on the eighteenth hole, and start visualizing your tee shot. Focus on this shot so intensely that no other image can sneak into your mental movie. At this moment, it doesn't matter what your putt looks like: you first have to get yourself in a position to even get to the green.

Walk up to the tee box, and capture the layout of the hole. Take a few deep breaths, calming yourself as you do. Visualize the flight path of the ball. Where is your target? Use your mind to zoom in on your first target and see exactly where you want the ball to land. Determine how you are going to play the hole. Tee up your ball, and go through your pre-shot routine. Address the ball, bring your club back, and remember your swing thought—"through the ball." Make your downswing, and send that ball. Wow! That felt incredible and sounded great, too. Watch the ball as it sails smoothly through the air and lands on the fairway. Good shot! You are definitely within reach of the green.

Take a step back, and let your partner play his tee shot. As you stand there watching him prepare and swing, take a few seconds to enjoy your last shot and then let it go. It's now in the past, and it's time to be in the present. Your partner hit a decent shot, and you both head down the fairway to your approach shot. You chat with your partner as you walk together. It has been a fun round so far, and you are both having a good time.

You walk up to your ball and see that you're in the primary rough, but you have a decent lie. Find your target on the green—the pin is the upper left corner of the green. Visualize your second shot landing softly on the green. Determine your distance and confidently grab your 7-iron. Visualize this shot again and again. Be sure to stay focused, bringing your mind back to the here and now.

Start your pre-shot routine. Take your position, make your takeaway, back swing, and then swing through the ball, keeping your head behind the ball and your hips open. Hear the ball smack the clubface; then watch it take flight. It lands on the edge of the green. Not exactly where you were aiming, but at least you're on. Taking a deep breath of relief, you feel the butterflies return to your stomach. Breathe in deeply a few more times, and repeat your mental mantra to yourself. You are so close. Keep your head about you, and take it one shot at a time.

Your partner has taken his second shot, and you meet up on the green. You are on the front side of the green and will be hitting uphill. Your distance to the hole is about twenty feet. You notice the green slopes toward the lake on the right. Walk around the green and get a good feel for it. See the line you want to take, and begin to see the ball run that path over and over again. Watch yourself from the outside and see how you strike the ball; notice your movement from the inside and feel the rhythm of your swing.

You're away and your partner takes his putt for birdie. He comes very close, but misses, and his ball rolls just past the hole. He's near enough and goes ahead and putts out.

It's just you on the green. Picture the putt a few more times; seal the look of it in your mind and the tempo of it in your muscles. Go through your pre-shot routine once again. Address the ball, and let your body listen to your brain. You stand over the ball. Your left eye is directly over the top of the ball. Take one last look down your line, feeling confident and committed to the putt. Focus on your tempo as you swing through the ball, connecting cleanly with the sweet spot of the putter. Watch the ball as it moves across the green in a perfect line toward the hole. See the rotation as it spins. See it drop into the hole. You did it! You birdied this hole and shot an overall score of 87, breaking 90 handily. What a great round! You feel relieved, satisfied, and excited as you just accomplished a goal you have been working toward for quite a while.

Mix It Up. Are you trying to break 100, 90, 80, or maybe even 70? What key things do you need to focus on to hit the score you want? Every article and instructor will prescribe something different—learn to use your driver correctly, control the ball flight, learn to roll the ball the right distance, avoid the snap hook, try this drill to make sure your swing path is inside out, practice another drill to make sure you hit your drives on the downswing.

All the advice is good, but it can become a bit dizzying. One basic principle to follow is to keep it simple. Don't try to fix everything at once. Remember to set your long-term goals (like breaking 80) and then figure out the short-term goals you need to reach to get you in a position to achieve your goal. Determine a few specific things you want to work on with each round or each visit to the practice range. Perhaps you want to work on keeping your shoulders and eyes level, on hitting from awkward lies, or on being sure your ball position is correct. Or maybe there's a mental component you want to work on: blocking out negative thoughts, staying in the present, or using your swing thought.

Whatever your desire, work on the short-term goals, knowing they are getting you closer to your long-term goal of breaking a certain score. Once you break the score you are working toward, reward yourself and then set new goals to move ahead.

O.P.E.N. Your Mind. Remember this feeling, this confidence, this satisfaction. Replay this routine in your head as part of your training regimen. See and feel every element of the different parts of a hole. Tune into the sounds, smells, and even tastes of performance. The more details you can visualize, the better your body can prepare.

As you're learning and perfecting your technique, use the following tips to O.P.E.N. yourself to improvement.

→ **Observe:** Did you visualize *internally* or *externally*? Some of both? What was most helpful from each view?

→ **Positive Practice:** If any negative images squeezed in, take a moment now to rewind your mental video, slow it down, and replace each mistake with a *positive* image. Repeat a cue word or action—maybe your mental mantra—to trigger this positive image. Replay the positive replacement at least three times to make sure it sticks in your mind.

→ **Experiment:** Can you mentally *slow down* your stroke speed and analyze your technique? Can you change the tempo of your swing? This is *control*. It takes practice! Often, slowing down your images and playing your "mental movie" frame by frame will allow you to control your performance in your mind.

→ **Notice:** Could you actually *feel* your body's movements, even slightly? This is the goal of guided imagery. Tune into the sounds, smells, and even tastes of performance. The more details you can visualize, the better your body can prepare. Visualizing yourself staying composed, focused on the present moment, and able to move on to the next shot is a great way to prepare for the unexpected.

Playing with Different Pairings

You may experience different feelings when playing with new people. Perhaps your anxiety level rises, or maybe you become more confident, or even cocky. Learning how to handle these feelings and to play on an even keel is the goal of this script.

Start by Relaxing

To begin, find a comfortable place to sit or lie down, and close your eyes. Take three deep abdominal breaths, exhaling slowly each time. As you exhale, imagine that tension throughout your body begins to flow away. Starting at your toes and working your way up to the top of your head, mentally scan your body for areas of tension. As you discover tension, contract the muscles in that area for ten seconds, then relax for fifteen seconds, and then contract for another ten seconds, followed by fifteen seconds of relaxation. Go through this contracting and relaxing cycle one more time. Continue scanning, looking for areas that need to be relaxed. Once you reach the top of your head, scan back down to your toes, noting any areas you may have missed. When you arrive back at your toes, take three more deep abdominal breaths. You are ready to visualize.

Visualize

You stand at the first hole of eighteen that you are playing with a partner who makes you feel unsettled and anxious. You are about to spend the next four to five hours with him, but you are trying to feel ready for it. He intimidates you, and you sense a real pressure to play well with him. You knew this was coming, and you have tried to prepare yourself for it during the past week. You want to play your game and not let him influence how you respond.

He is the first to tee off. You watch as he lines up his target, takes a few practice swings, then steps up to the ball and hits a solid tee shot right down the middle of the fairway. He lands in great position and will definitely make it to the green on his next shot.

You're up next. You sense a nervous tension building in your muscles, and a worried thought creeps into your head. You pull it together quickly, reminding yourself that you are here to play *your* game, not his. Take a few deep breaths as you scope your target and start your pre-shot routine. You take your swing and land on the fairway. You aren't quite as close to the green as your partner is, but you have hit a good shot and are still in position to play onto the green with your next shot. As you walk to where your ball lies, try to enjoy the game—release yourself from the stress and anxiety of playing with this individual. Play your own game, repeat your mental mantra to yourself, and remember that what he does is out of your control. You can only control your thoughts and reactions. Commit fully to each shot you take, and choose to accept the results. Also choose to accept the results of your partner and to let him play his game.

You come up to your approach shot confidently. Your concentration is on this shot. You evaluate the distance to the pin, where the pin stands on the green, the wind, and the angle of the green, and you determine your target. Select your club and once again methodically run through your pre-shot routine. Your swing feels great as you follow through and send the ball directly to your target. It lands on the green, and you are in position for birdie.

Mix It Up. Imagine what it would be like to play a round of golf with Tiger Woods. What feelings arise from that thought? Intimidation, excitement, fear, nervousness, giddiness? It might seem like a dream come true, but for many tour players, playing with Tiger can be distracting and pressured. Or perhaps you're playing with your boss or an important client. How do you make sure you play your game?

Picture yourself at your home course, and consider the different partners or groups with whom you have played. Do you have a favorite person with whom you enjoy playing? What is the worst pairing you have ever played? How do other players view being paired with you?

O.P.E.N. Your Mind. Remember this feeling, this confidence, this satisfaction. Replay this routine in your head as part of your training regimen. See and feel every element of the different parts of a hole. Tune into the sounds, smells, and even tastes of performance. The more details you can visualize, the better your body can prepare.

As you're learning and perfecting your technique, use the following tips to O.P.E.N. yourself to improvement.

- → **Observe:** Did you visualize *internally* or *externally*? Some of both? What was most helpful from each view?
- → **Positive Practice:** If any negative images squeezed in, take a moment now to rewind your mental video, slow it down, and replace each mistake with a *positive* image. Repeat a cue word or action—maybe your mental mantra—to trigger this positive image. Replay the positive replacement at least three times to make sure it sticks in your mind.
- → **Experiment:** Can you mentally *slow down* your stroke speed and analyze your technique? Can you change the tempo of your swing? This is *control.* It takes practice! Often, slowing down your images and playing your "mental movie" frame by frame allows you to control your performance in your mind.
- → **Notice:** Could you actually *feel* your body's movements, even slightly? This is the goal of guided imagery. Tune into the sounds, smells, and even tastes of performance. The more details you can visualize, the better your body can prepare. Visualizing yourself staying composed, focused on the present moment, and able to move on to the next shot is a great way to prepare for the unexpected.

Playing a New Course

The challenges of playing on an unfamiliar course are obvious. But overcoming those challenges may be trickier. Use this script to help you mentally play the new course so that when you actually arrive, you have the confidence of having already played it.

Start by Relaxing

To begin, find a comfortable place to sit or lie down, and close your eyes. Take three deep abdominal breaths, exhaling slowly each time. As you exhale, imagine that tension throughout your body begins to flow away. Starting at your toes and working your way up to the top of your head, mentally scan your body for areas of tension. As you discover tension, contract the muscles in that area for ten seconds, then relax for fifteen seconds, and then contract for another ten seconds, followed by fifteen seconds of relaxation. Go through this contracting and relaxing cycle one more time. Continue scanning, looking for areas that need to be relaxed. Once you reach the top of your head, scan back down to your toes, noting any areas you may have missed. When you arrive back at your toes, take three more deep abdominal breaths. You are ready to visualize.

Visualize

It's a beautiful morning, and you drive to meet your friends for an early tee time. They have been talking about playing this course with you for quite a while, and all four of you were finally able to find a time that worked. You are looking forward to the round, but you are a little uncertain about the course. It's known to be a tough course, and although your friends really enjoy playing there, it's your first time and you really do not know what to expect.

You arrive at the course, pick up a bucket of balls and a scorecard from the clubhouse, and head over to the practice range. While doing a few warm-up stretches, you look over the scorecard and begin to gain a vision for the course. There is a tight dogleg on the third hole, a very narrow fairway with bunkering on both sides on the seventh, a downhill tee shot on fifteen, and a blind fairway on sixteen, just to name a few tricky spots. You have your work cut out for you, but are excited to play and feel up for the challenge.

As you take the time to stretch and do some deep breathing—before even swinging a club—begin visualizing each hole as you see it on the scorecard. Think through the clubs you will use from the tees as well as what you need for fairway shots and the greens. Also take into consideration the current weather conditions and how that might affect which club you need to use. Jot down notes as you plan for your round.

Your friends start arriving at the range as you are going through your preparations. You talk with them for a few minutes, and then finish up your visualization session.

As you feel ready, step up and start hitting through your clubs. Think back to the visualization you just did, and work to remember when you might potentially use the different clubs on the course. Visualize a specific target out on the range with each swing you take. Focus in on it, and imagine you are actually playing a hole. Feel your rhythm as you swing the club. Tune into that rhythm, and imprint that cadence in your muscles and in your mind. After you are done at the driving range, head over to the practice green and get a feel for how fast the greens are here. See yourself in different putting scenarios and putt accordingly, taking your time to line things up and get an accurate read on the green.

You are finished warming up by the time your foursome is called, and you are ready to have a fun time and great round with your friends. You are first to tee off, and you immediately put your visualization practice into action. You know what to expect from the first hole and what club you want to use for your tee shot. Grab your club, tee up your ball, take a step back behind the ball, and find your target. Visualize the shot and the flight path of the ball. Come around and address the ball, going through your pre-shot routine. You make your backswing and . . .

Mix It Up. See the resulting shot in your mind. Also consider the scenario where you are playing a tournament at a new course you have never seen or played before. How can you modify this script to be appropriate for that situation? Perhaps before the tournament you would find a scorecard, or visit the course's website, and check out a course overview for an idea of how each hole plays and rehearse it regularly beforehand. If it's a popular course, there may be photos online that give you an actual visual idea of what you'll be seeing. Use these tools to help create good images of the course that can help you effectively visualize a round.

O.P.E.N. Your Mind. Remember this feeling, this confidence, this satisfaction. Replay this routine in your head as part of your training regimen. See and feel every element of the different parts of a hole. Tune into the sounds, smells, and even tastes of performance. The more details you can visualize, the better your body can prepare.

As you're learning and perfecting your technique, use the following tips to O.P.E.N. yourself to improvement.

→ **Observe:** Did you visualize *internally* or *externally*? Some of both?
→ **Positive Practice:** If any negative images squeezed in, take a moment now to rewind your mental video and replace them with *positive* images. Repeat a cue word or action—maybe your mental mantra—to trigger this positive image. Replay the positive replacement at least three times to make sure it sticks in your mind.

→ **Experiment:** Can you *slow down* your stroke speed and analyze your technique? Can you change the tempo of your swing? This is *control*. It takes practice! Often, slowing down your images and playing your "mental movie" frame by frame allows you to control your performance in your mind.

→ **Notice:** Could you actually *feel* your body's movements, even slightly? This is the goal of guided imagery. Tune into the sounds, smells, and even tastes of performance. The more details you can visualize, the better your body can prepare. Visualizing yourself staying composed, focused on the present moment, and able to move on to the next shot is a great way to prepare for the unexpected.

*Design Your Own
Visualization Scripts*

The previous chapter gave you nine different scenarios to visualize. Each of these scenes had circumstances that you may or may not run into during your next round of golf. For instance, when you are teeing off, you may not be as nervous about others' opinions as was the golfer in the script. You may, instead, be more concerned with implementing your new swing. You may feel differently under pressure to play for a certain score than does the golfer in the example. Your course will most likely have different hazards than the course in the script about playing from the rough. These samples were designed to show you what you should *generally* try to visualize. Designing your own script allows you to tailor, on each stroke, each image to your personal needs as a player.

To be able to visualize exactly what you need, when you need, it's essential that you be able to create your own imagery scripts at the drop of a hat. This chapter gives you the necessary guidance to learn where to start, what to include, and how to put it all together in your mind. Using these worksheets as a reference should provide you with a springboard from which you can visualize any hole, shot, or circumstance at any time.

Creating imagery scripts customized to your particular round, score, strengths, weaknesses, or your standing in the game can be an extremely valuable tool. Keep both the principle of dominant thought and the imagination principle in mind as you prepare your scripts, knowing that by replaying any script regularly in your mind, you are preparing your body to respond physically in a similar pattern to what you are visualizing. Being able to create your own script allows you to prepare for and achieve your peak performance on the course.

Ahead, you will find three worksheets. Each worksheet is set up to get you thinking about the specific details your images will include. Go through them one at a time, using each worksheet for a different scenario. For each worksheet we provide a potential subject for your script, but you are not limited to that topic. The choice is yours. Once you've completed each worksheet, you should be able to move into creating images in your head, without writing down any prompts. But this is one step ahead of where you are now. First start with the following questions.

WORKSHEET 1

STEP 1

Defining exactly what you are trying to achieve in each script is an important place to begin. For your first scenario, consider writing a script that takes you through your pre-shot routine. If you would rather focus on a different part of your game, you may write your script for that instead. For every scene you visualize, create a script unique to how you practice and play.

What am I trying to accomplish in my script? What specifically do I want it to be about?

_____

_____

STEP 2

Now that you know what your purpose is in creating the script, think about what key words or phrases and actions you need to incorporate. Which senses will you activate, and how are they involved in this experience? Perhaps it's the smell of your leather glove, the feel of your grip on your club, or the look of the pin on the green. Who are the characters of your script? Are you alone, or are others involved? Consider your setting as you construct the stage for your mental imagery to take place.

Define your details:

Sights: _____

Sounds: _____

Temperature: _____

Bodily feelings: _____

Tastes: _____

Smells: _____

Position of other players: _____

Location of hazards: _____

Pressure source: _____

Score: _____

Other details: _____

STEP 3

You now have the backbone of your script in place and are ready to bring
things together. As you write your script, try to use words that powerfully
describe your images and convey energy and confidence. For example, you
may say, "I approach the ball with strength and confidence, sharply focusing
my eyes on my target." Review the sample scripts in this book to get an idea of
how to construct your own. Additionally, sit down with your pro or coach and
get his or her suggestions for what you should be reviewing in your mind.

*Write out your script on a sheet of paper. The exercise should be long enough
to create a vivid experience of the critical elements of your performance.*

WORKSHEET 2

STEP 1

Remember that it is important to start by defining the objective of your script. For this second script, we recommend focusing on a specific skill. Perhaps you'd like to work on your chip shot or putting. Decide which skill you would like to visualize.

What am I trying to accomplish in my script? What specifically do I want it to be about?

_____

_____

STEP 2

Now that you know what your purpose is in creating the script, think about what key words or phrases and actions you need to incorporate. Which senses will you activate, and how are they involved in this experience? What specific elements should be included? You may want to consider the feel of the green beneath your feet, the weight of your club in your hands, the lie of the ball, or a firm wrist. Who are the characters of your script? Are you alone, or are others involved? Consider your setting as you construct the stage for your mental imagery to take place.

Define your details:

Sights: _____

Sounds: _____

Temperature: _____

Bodily feelings: _____

Tastes: _____

Smells: _____

Position of other players: _____

Location of hazards: _____

Pressure source: _____

Score: _____

Other details: _____

STEP 3

You now have the backbone of your script in place and are ready to bring things together. As you write your script, try to use words that powerfully describe your images and convey energy and confidence. For example, you may say, "Level shoulders, soft hands, even swing." Review the sample scripts in this book to get an idea of how to construct your own. Additionally, sit down with your pro or coach and get his or her suggestions for what you should be reviewing in your mind.

Write out your script on a sheet of paper. The exercise should be long enough to create a vivid experience of the critical elements of your performance.

WORKSHEET 3

STEP 1

For your third script, we encourage you to create a plan for recovering from a bad shot. If there is a script you'd rather create, please do so. Always begin by defining the objective of your script and what you would like to achieve.

What am I trying to accomplish in my script? What specifically do I want it to be about?

_____

_____

STEP 2

Now that you know what your purpose is in creating the script, think about what key words or phrases and actions you need to incorporate. Which senses will you activate, and how are they involved in this experience? Will you evoke feelings of frustration or disappointment? How will your self-talk be described? Do you feel tension in your muscles? Who are the characters of your script? Are you alone, or are others involved? Consider your setting as you construct the stage for your mental imagery to take place.

Define your details:

Sights: _____

Sounds: _____

Temperature: _____

Bodily feelings: _____

Tastes: _____

Smells: _____

Position of other players: _____

Location of hazards: _____

Pressure source: _____

Score: _____

Other details: _____

STEP 3

You now have the backbone of your script in place and are ready to bring things together. As you write your script, try to use words that powerfully describe your images and convey energy and confidence. For example, you may say, "I breathe deeply, inhaling energy and exhaling frustration." Review the sample scripts in this book to get an idea of how to construct your own. Additionally, sit down with your pro or coach and get his or her suggestions for what you should be reviewing in your mind.

Write out your script on a sheet of paper. The exercise should be long enough to create a vivid experience of the critical elements of your performance.

START BY RELAXING

Always begin with relaxation, especially when you're first becoming familiar with imagery. Use the following relaxation exercise as a guide.

To begin, find a comfortable place to sit or lie down, and close your eyes. Take three deep abdominal breaths, exhaling slowly each time. As you exhale, imagine that tension throughout your body begins to flow away. Starting at your toes and working your way up to the top of your head, scan your body for areas of tension. As you discover tension, contract the muscles in that area for ten seconds, then relax for fifteen seconds, and then contract for another ten seconds, followed by fifteen seconds of relaxation. Go through this contracting and relaxing cycle one more time. Continue scanning, looking for areas that need to be relaxed. Once you reach the top of your head, scan back down to your toes, noting any areas you may have missed. When you arrive back at your toes, take three more deep abdominal breaths. You are ready to visualize.

Always starting with the relaxation instructions, read all the way through each of your scripts. As you improve at visualizing, you'll be able to employ a shortened version of relaxation and imagery to trigger your optimal physical response.

TAKING THE NEXT STEPS

Consider recording yourself as you read your script aloud; then use this audio version of your script intermittently with reading the written script. Also, if you listen to music between holes, try reviewing the script while listening to that tune.

Using these scripts as a springboard, you can dive right in and create more of your own mental imagery scripts for specific competitive situations. Your images are in your control—do in your mind what you want to do on the links, and you're on your way! You may prefer to write out your scripts and read them in preparation for use. But with practice, you'll feel comfortable mentally creating scripts on the spot to serve your specific needs.

*How Far
Have You Come?*

The questions in this section are designed to assess how far you have come in applying the techniques of *Golfing with Your Eyes Closed*. By honestly answering the questions, you will discover what specific areas you can work on to improve your mental acuity as a golfer. Begin the assessments in this chapter after you have completed the rest of the book and have been using visualization in your golf game for about a month. Also, take the time periodically to reassess your visualization skill and track your improvement by answering the Self-Assessment questions from the Introduction using the Self-Assessment Scorecard.

At those times, the fairways look wider, the hole looks bigger, and you just can't wait to get to the next shot because you know you'll hit it well. It's the way golf is played in Heaven.

—*PETER JACOBSEN*[1]

FOLLOW-UP ASSESSMENT

1. Do you use both internal and external imagery now? Have you noticed whether one is more effective for you in certain tasks? Which helps you most in teeing off? In recovering after a poor shot? In correcting a swing error?

_____

_____

_____

_____

Remember the benefits of both: external imagery helps detect and correct mistakes, while internal imagery re-creates the feeling of performance.

2. How often do you visualize? In which instances, specifically, do you image?

_____

_____

_____

_____

Remember, the more often you visualize, the better chance you have of strengthening your muscle memory. Visualize before a tough shot and after a great one to imprint the correct mechanics on your brain.

3. Where are you when you are able to visualize most clearly? In bed? Approaching the ball? Walking from one hole to the next?

_____

_____

_____

_____

_____

_____

If you visualize best off the course, how can you replicate those comfortable surroundings on the course in a round of golf?

_____

4. How well can you apply imagery to practice and competitive games?

_____

_____

_____

_____

_____

_____

Remember, the more you practice, the easier it gets. For best results, be sure to visualize both in practice and in competition.

5. What still needs improvement in your imagery ability?

_____

_____

_____

_____

How will you go about achieving this progress? Look back through the summaries of the chapters to stir your memory about other techniques you might try.

_____

_____

_____

_____

Remember, mastering the mental game takes constant practice, just like your physical game.

6. How consistent are you with your pre-shot routine? Do you always do the same thing before each stroke? Have you made acceptance part of your routine? Define any changes you wish to make in your routine.

_____

_____

_____

_____

_____

Remember, the more consistent your pre-performance routine, the more you can rely on that structure to keep you in check under pressure on the course.

7. What swing thoughts are you using most often?

_____

_____

_____

_____

Remember, a verbal or physical cue can trigger positive images and feelings.

8. What is your mental mantra? Perhaps you have tried out one or two different phrases. Which one comes most naturally?

_____

_____

_____

Remember, use your mental mantra to motivate, encourage, and energize you.

9. In terms of relaxation techniques, what do you find yourself relying on
when you are nervous?

_____

_____

_____

_____

_____

_____

*Remember, you may use any combination of relaxation imagery, progres-
sive muscle relaxation, controlled breathing, and the like.*

10. How confident would you say you are as a golfer? Are there some specific
areas in which you would like to be more confident?

_____

_____

_____

What three goals might you set to help you gain confidence in those areas?

1. _____

_____

2. _____

_____

3. _____

_____

Remember, visualize what you do well to boost your confidence. You can convince your brain that you can do it by mentally rehearsing.

11. How well are you able to replace or cover up negative thoughts with positive images? In which instances have you caught yourself worrying or overanalyzing and then used a cue to trigger a positive replacement image?

_____

_____

_____

_____

_____

Remember, thought-replacement techniques include picture perfect, thought stopping, thought changing, and countering.

12. Have you been keeping track of your daily affirmations? If so, where do you keep them?

_____

_____

_____

_____

_____

Remember, write down your positive affirmations and keep them with you to review on the course. If you haven't already, start a little journal of positive thoughts.

13. Have you noticed any change in your level of nervousness? What do you think has been the cause of the change?

_____

_____

_____

_____

Remember, nerves are caused by a variety of factors. Getting a grip on your nerves begins with identifying their causes.

14. Have you found yourself actively noticing which triggers, relevant or irrelevant, tend to grab your attention? Which irrelevant triggers have caught you?

_____

_____

_____

_____

_____

How will you attempt to block out these irrelevant triggers and focus only on the relevant ones?

_____

_____

_____

_____

_____

Remember, you want to focus only on the things you can control. Regulating your energy level will help you reach this zone of concentration.

15. What three positive things did you take from the last round you played?

1. _____

_____

2. _____

_____

3. _____

_____

Remember to always leave the course with three positive thoughts about your day's game, no matter how you played. Keeping even small good

*aspects of your game in the forefront of your mind builds your confidence
and motivation.*

16. Which specific techniques have you tried to assist you in refocusing after a
distracting thought, bad shot, or lousy front nine?

_____

_____

_____

_____

_____

*Remember, you may mentally prepare with the refocusing script, attentional
cues, mindfulness, one-point focus, and competition simulations.*

17. Did you ever feel you were starting to choke, but used visualization to help
you remain focused on what you could control? What were you thinking?

_____

_____

_____

_____

_____

Remember, focus on the relevant triggers.

18. Can you identify at least one situation where you consciously made the
choice to believe in your club choice and mentally block out the alternatives? How did this affect the subsequent shot?

_____

_____

_____

_____

Remember, your belief in your choice can be more important than the actually accuracy of your choice. Weigh your options and stick to your decision so that your only focus when you address the ball is your mental mantra.

19. Have you found that your motivation to play golf has changed by reading and applying the techniques in this manual? Why do you play golf?

Remember, you may be intrinsically or extrinsically motivated to play. To boost intrinsic motivation, visualize your dream round.

20. Have you noticed where your attributions for success and failure fall? How much of an impact do you think luck and hard work have on your game?

Remember, take ownership of your motivation by focusing on the parts of your game you can control.

21. What long-term M.A.S.T.E.R. goal are you aiming to achieve?

_____

_____

_____

_____

_____

_____

Remember, M.A.S.T.E.R. stands for measurable, adaptable, specific, time-bound, encouraging, and realistic.

22. List three short-term or intermediate M.A.S.T.E.R. goals you have achieved during the past month.

1. _____

   _____

2. _____

   _____

3. _____

   _____

Remember to take the time to review your goals weekly to make sure you stay on track and motivated.

23. Which goals are next on your list?

_____

_____

_____

_____

_____

_____

Remember to try to anticipate any speed bumps you may encounter on your path to success. Then smooth out these bumps before you reach them, by identifying what you can do to overcome them.

24. Where have you written your goals and posted them?

_____

_____

_____

Remember, ink it, don't just think it!

25. Where have you used imagery and visualization off the golf course? How has it helped you?

_____

_____

_____

_____

_____

_____

Remember, visualization is a mental skill that applies to golf as well as to other performance areas in your life. Use it often!

26. Reward yourself for getting this far! Take the time to pat yourself on the back and recognize your efforts in enhancing your mental toughness. Congratulations!

REFERENCES

Introduction

1. Criswell Freeman, ed., *The Golfer's Book of Wisdom* (Nashville: Walnut Grove Press, 1995), 62.

Chapter 1

1. Mark Frost, "The Greatest Game Ever Played," DVD, directed by Bill Paxton (Burbank, CA: Walt Disney Studios, 1995).
2. Wade Pearse, "Visualization for Golf—Feeling with Your Mind's Eye," golf-mental-game-coach.com/visualization.html.
3. Quotes to Inspire You. "Imagination," Jack Nicklaus, cybernation.com/victory/quotations/subjects/quotes_imagination.html.
4. Mary Jane Miner, Greg A. Shelley, and Keith P. Henschen, *Moving Toward Your Potential: The Athlete's Guide to Peak Performance*, 2nd ed. (Farmington, UT: Performance Publications, 1995).
5. Edmund Jacobson, *You Must Relax* (New York: Whittlesey House, 1934).
6. Stephen M. Kosslyn, *Image and the Brain: The Resolution of the Imagery Debate* (Cambridge, MA: MIT Press, 1996).
7. Greg A. Shelley, "Psychological Perspectives of Sport," lecture (Ithaca College, Ithaca, NY, 2000).
8. Haythum R. Khalid, "Famous Quotes About Visualization," famous-quotes.com/topic.php?tid=1278.
9. Criswell Freeman, ed., *The Golfer's Book of Wisdom* (Nashville: Walnut Grove Press, 1995), 86.

Chapter 2

1. Edmund J. Bourne, *The Anxiety and Phobia Workbook* (Oakland, CA: New Harbinger Publications, 1990), 70.
2. Edmund J. Bourne, *The Anxiety and Phobia Workbook* (Oakland, CA: New Harbinger Publications, 1990), 72–74.
3. Tiger Woods, *How I Play Golf* (New York: Warner Books, 2001).
4. Butch Harmon, "Swing to a Finish: One Simple Thought to Hitting It Fat," *Golf Digest*, July 2007, golfdigest.com/instruction/swing/2007/07/butchharmon_0707.
5. Hank Haney, "Fix Your Pre-Shot Routine: Approach from Behind, Not the Side" *Golf Digest*, April 2008, golfdigest.com/instruction/longgame/consistency/haney_gd0804.
6. Bob Rotella, "How Padraig Harrington Changed His Mental Approach and Won the British Open." *Golf Digest 59*, no. 6 (May 2008): 124–127.

7. Butch Harmon, "Swing to a Finish: One Simple Thought to Hitting It Fat," *Golf Digest*, July 2007, golfdigest.com/instruction/swing/2007/07/ butchharmon_0707

8. Jeff Rendell, "To Hit Straight, Play That Funk-y Music," *Washington Post*, May 5, 2006, washingtonpost.com/wp-dyn/content/article/2006/05/05/ AR2006050500574.html.

9. Hunki Yun, "Lessons from Golf's Greatest Swing," *Golf Digest*, 1996, golfdigest.co.za/instruction/html/instruction3.php.

10. Criswell Freeman, ed., *The Golfer's Book of Wisdom* (Nashville: Walnut Grove Press, 1995), 92.

Chapter 3

1. Susan A. Jackson and Mihaly Csikszentmihalyi, *Flow in Sports: The Keys to Optimal Experiences and Performance* (Champaign, IL: Human Kinetics, 1999).

2. Robert S. Weinberg and Daniel Gould, *Foundations of Exercise & Sport Psychology*, 2nd ed. (Champaign, IL: Human Kinetics, 1999).

3. Richard H. Cox, *Sport Psychology Concepts and Applications*, 2nd ed. (Dubuque, IA: Wm. C. Brown, 1990).

4. Brendan Hackett, *Success from Within* (Limerick, Ireland: National Coaching & Training Centre, 1998).

5. Terry Orlick, *In Pursuit of Excellence*, 3rd ed. (Champaign, IL: Human Kinetics, 2000).

6. Lew Hardy, Graham Jones, and Daniel Gould, *Understanding Psychological Preparation for Sport* (New York: John Wiley & Sons, 1996).

7. Daniel L. Wann, *Sport Psychology* (Upper Saddle River, NJ: Prentice-Hall, 1997).

8. Robert S. Weinberg and Daniel Gould, *Foundations of Exercise and Sport Psychology*, 2nd ed. (Champaign, IL: Human Kinetics, 1999).

9. Robert S. Weinberg and Daniel Gould, *Foundations of Exercise and Sport Psychology*, 2nd ed. (Champaign, IL: Human Kinetics, 1999).

10. Daniel L. Wann, *Sport Psychology* (Upper Saddle River, NJ: Prentice-Hall, 1997).

11. Daniel L. Wann, *Sport Psychology* (Upper Saddle River, NJ: Prentice-Hall, 1997).

12. Robert S. Weinberg and Daniel Gould, *Foundations of Exercise and Sport Psychology*, 2nd ed. (Champaign, IL: Human Kinetics, 1999).

13. Robert S. Weinberg and Daniel Gould, *Foundations of Exercise and Sport Psychology*, 2nd ed. (Champaign, IL: Human Kinetics, 1999).

14. Criswell Freeman, ed., *The Golfer's Book of Wisdom* (Nashville: Walnut Grove Press, 1995), 112.

15. Nate Zinsser, Linda Bunker, and Jean M. Williams, "Cognitive Techniques for Building Confidence and Enhancing Performance," in *Applied Sport Psychology*, ed. Jean M. Williams, 270–295 (Mountain View, CA: Mayfield, 1998).

16. Terry Orlick, *Psyching for Sport: Mental Training for Athletes* (Champaign, IL: Leisure Press, 1986).

17. Nate Zinsser, Linda Bunker, and Jean M. Williams, "Cognitive Techniques for Building Confidence and Enhancing Performance," in *Applied Sport Psychology*, ed. Jean M. Williams, 270–295 (Mountain View, CA: Mayfield, 1998).

18. Robert S. Weinberg and Daniel Gould, *Foundations of Exercise and Sport Psychology*, 2nd ed. (Champaign, IL: Human Kinetics, 1999).

19. Manfred Tschan, "Motor Development and Skill Learning," lecture (Newberg, OR: George Fox University, 2000).

20. Nate Zinsser, Linda Bunker, and Jean M. Williams, "Cognitive Techniques for Building Confidence and Enhancing Performance," in *Applied Sport Psychology*, ed. Jean M. Williams, 270–295 (Mountain View, CA: Mayfield, 1998).

21. Nate Zinsser, Linda Bunker, and Jean M. Williams, "Cognitive Techniques for Building Confidence and Enhancing Performance," in *Applied Sport Psychology*, ed. Jean M. Williams, 270–295 (Mountain View, CA: Mayfield, 1998).

22. Robert S. Weinberg and Daniel Gould, *Foundations of Exercise and Sport Psychology*, 2nd ed. (Champaign, IL: Human Kinetics, 1999).

23. Nate Zinsser, Linda Bunker, and Jean M. Williams, "Cognitive Techniques for Building Confidence and Enhancing Performance," in *Applied Sport Psychology*, ed. Jean M. Williams, 270–295 (Mountain View, CA: Mayfield, 1998).

24. Linda J. Bunker, "Golf: Sport Psychology Challenges," in *The Sport Psychologist's Handbook: A Guide for Sport-Specific Performance Enhancement*, ed. Joaquin Dosil, 301–320 (West Sussex, England: John Wiley & Sons, 2006).

25. Criswell Freeman, ed., *The Golfer's Book of Wisdom* (Nashville: Walnut Grove Press, 1995), 89.

26. Nate Zinsser, Linda Bunker, and Jean M. Williams, "Cognitive Techniques for Building Confidence and Enhancing Performance," in *Applied Sport Psychology*, ed. Jean M. Williams, 270–295 (Mountain View, CA: Mayfield, 1998).

27. Robert S. Weinberg and Daniel Gould, *Foundations of Exercise and Sport Psychology*, 2nd ed. (Champaign, IL: Human Kinetics, 1999).

28. Nate Zinsser, Linda Bunker, and Jean M. Williams, "Cognitive Techniques for Building Confidence and Enhancing Performance," in *Applied Sport Psychology*, ed. Jean M. Williams, 270–295 (Mountain View, CA: Mayfield, 1998).

29. Linda J. Bunker, "Golf: Sport Psychology Challenges," in *The Sport Psychologist's Handbook: A Guide for Sport-Specific Performance Enhancement*, ed. Joaquin Dosil, 301–320 (West Sussex, England: John Wiley & Sons, 2006).

30. Dan S. Kirschenbaum, *Mind Matters: Seven Steps to Smarter Sport Performance* (New York: Cooper Publishing Group, 1997).

31. Nate Zinsser, Linda Bunker, and Jean M. Williams, "Cognitive Techniques for Building Confidence and Enhancing Performance," in *Applied Sport Psychology*, ed. Jean M. Williams, 270–295 (Mountain View, CA: Mayfield, 1998).

32. Nate Zinsser, Linda Bunker, and Jean M. Williams, "Cognitive Techniques for Building Confidence and Enhancing Performance," in *Applied Sport Psychology*, ed. Jean M. Williams, 270–295 (Mountain View, CA: Mayfield, 1998).

Chapter 4

1. Robert M. Nideffer, *The Inner Athlete* (New York: Crowell, 1976).

2. Criswell Freeman, ed., *The Golfer's Book of Wisdom* (Nashville: Walnut Grove Press, 1995), 109.

3. Mark H. Anshel, *Sport Psychology: From Theory to Practice*, 3rd ed. (Scottsdale, AZ: Benjamin-Cummings Publishing Company, 1997).

4. Leonard D. Zaichkowsky and Amy Baltzell, "Arousal and Performance," in *Handbook of Sport Psychology*, 2nd ed., eds. Robert N. Singer, Heather A. Hausenblas, and Christopher Janelle, 319–339 (New York: John Wiley & Sons, 2001).

5. Edmund J. Bourne, *The Anxiety and Phobia Workbook* (Oakland, CA: New Harbinger Publications, 1990).

6. Edmund J. Bourne, *The Anxiety and Phobia Workbook* (Oakland, CA: New Harbinger Publications, 1990).

7. Criswell Freeman, ed., *The Golfer's Book of Wisdom* (Nashville: Walnut Grove Press, 1995), 87.

8. Edmund J. Bourne, *The Anxiety and Phobia Workbook* (Oakland, CA: New Harbinger Publications, 1990), 69.

9. Edmund J. Bourne, *The Anxiety and Phobia Workbook* (Oakland, CA: New Harbinger Publications, 1990), 70.

10. Edmund J. Bourne, *The Anxiety and Phobia Workbook* (Oakland, CA: New Harbinger Publications, 1990), 70.

11. Edmund J. Bourne, *The Anxiety and Phobia Workbook* (Oakland, CA: New Harbinger Publications, 1990), 70.

12. Robert S. Weinberg and Daniel Gould, *Foundations of Exercise and Sport Psychology*, 2nd ed. (Champaign, IL: Human Kinetics, 1999).

13. Robert S. Weinberg and Daniel Gould, *Foundations of Exercise and Sport Psychology*, 2nd ed. (Champaign, IL: Human Kinetics, 1999).

14. Andrea Schmid and Erik Peper. "Strategies for Training Concentration," in *Applied Sport Psychology*, ed. Jean M. Williams, 316–328. (Mountain View, CA: Mayfield, 1998).

15. Robert S. Weinberg and Daniel Gould, *Foundations of Exercise and Sport Psychology*, 2nd ed. (Champaign, IL: Human Kinetics, 1999).

16. Robert S. Weinberg and Daniel Gould, *Foundations of Exercise and Sport Psychology*, 2nd ed. (Champaign, IL: Human Kinetics, 1999).

17. Peter Jacobsen, *Buried Lies* (New York: G. P. Putnam's Sons, 1993), 47.

18. Amy Moulton, "Model Showing the Narrowing of Attentional Focus That Occurs with Increasing Mental Activation," paper presented in Applications of Sport Psychology course (Ithaca, NY, 2001).

19. Peter Jacobsen, *Buried Lies* (New York: G. P. Putnam's Sons, 1993), 79.

20. Terry Orlick, *In Pursuit of Excellence*, 3rd ed. (Champaign, IL: Human Kinetics, 2000).

21. Peter Jacobsen, *Buried Lies* (New York: G. P. Putnam's Sons, 1993).

22. Terry Orlick, *In Pursuit of Excellence*, 3rd ed. (Champaign, IL: Human Kinetics, 2000).

23. Robert S. Weinberg and Daniel Gould, *Foundations of Exercise and Sport Psychology*, 2nd ed. (Champaign, IL: Human Kinetics, 1999).

24. Andrea Schmid and Erik Peper, "Strategies for Training Concentration," in *Applied Sport Psychology*, ed. Jean M. Williams, 316–328 (Mountain View, CA: Mayfield, 1998).

25. Nate Zinsser, Linda Bunker, and Jean M. Williams, "Cognitive Techniques for Building Confidence and Enhancing Performance," in *Applied Sport Psychology*, ed. Jean M. Williams, 270–295 (Mountain View, CA: Mayfield, 1998).

26. Andrea Schmid and Erik Peper, "Strategies for Training Concentration," in *Applied Sport Psychology*, ed. Jean M. Williams, 316–328. (Mountain View, CA: Mayfield, 1998).

27. Dede Owens and Linda K. Bunker, *Advanced Golf: Steps to Success* (Champaign, IL: Human Kinetics, 1992), 323–324.

28. Andrea Schmid and Erik Peper, "Strategies for Training Concentration," in *Applied Sport Psychology*, ed. Jean M. Williams, 316–328 (Mountain View, CA: Mayfield, 1998).

29. Criswell Freeman, ed., *The Golfer's Book of Wisdom* (Nashville: Walnut Grove Press, 1995), 17.

30. Mark H. Anshel, *Sport Psychology: From Theory to Practice*, 3rd ed. (Scottsdale, AZ: Benjamin-Cummings Publishing Company, 1997).

Chapter 5

1. Johnmarshall Reeve, *Understanding Motivation and Emotion*, 2nd ed. (Fort Worth, TX: Harcourt Brace College, 1997).

2. Eugene F. Gauron, *Mental Training for Peak Performance* (Lansing, NY: Sport Science Associates, 1984).

3. Yves Chantal and others, "Motivation and Elite Performance: An Exploratory Investigation with Bulgarian Athletes." *International Journal of Sport Psychology* 27, no. 2 (1996): 173–182.

4. Diane L. Gill, *Psychological Dynamics of Sport and Exercise*, 2nd ed. (Champaign, IL: Human Kinetics, 2000).

5. Diane L. Gill, *Psychological Dynamics of Sport and Exercise*, 2nd ed. (Champaign, IL: Human Kinetics, 2000).

6. Greg A. Shelley, "Psychological Perspectives of Sport," lecture (Ithaca College, Ithaca, NY, 2000).

7. Diane L. Gill, *Psychological Dynamics of Sport and Exercise*, 2nd ed. (Champaign, IL: Human Kinetics, 2000).

8. Criswell Freeman, ed., *The Golfer's Book of Wisdom* (Nashville: Walnut Grove Press, 1995), 139.

9. Greg A. Shelley, "Psychological Perspectives of Sport," lecture (Ithaca College, Ithaca, NY, 2000).

10. Greg A. Shelley, "Psychological Perspectives of Sport," lecture (Ithaca College, Ithaca, NY, 2000).

11. Daniel Gould, "Goal Setting for Peak Performance," in *Applied Sport Psychology*, ed. Jean M. Williams, 182–196 (Mountain View, CA: Mayfield, 1998).

12. Mary Lou Retton, *Mary Lou Retton's Gateways to Happiness: Seven Ways to a More Peaceful, More Prosperous, More Satisfying Life* (New York: Broadway Books, 2000), 144.

13. Greg A. Shelley, "Psychological Perspectives of Sport," lecture (Ithaca College, Ithaca, NY, 2000).

Chapter 6

1. Criswell Freeman, ed., *The Golfer's Book of Wisdom* (Nashville: Walnut Grove Press, 1995), 126.

2. Criswell Freeman, ed., *The Golfer's Book of Wisdom* (Nashville: Walnut Grove Press, 1995), 24.

3. Criswell Freeman, ed., *The Golfer's Book of Wisdom* (Nashville: Walnut Grove Press, 1995), 52.

Chapter 9

1. Peter Jacobsen, *Buried Lies* (New York: G. P. Putnam's Sons, 1993), 32.

BIBLIOGRAPHY

Anshel, Mark H. *Sport Psychology: From Theory to Practice.* 3rd ed. Scottsdale, AZ: Benjamin-Cummings Publishing Company, 1997.

Bourne, Edmund J. *The Anxiety and Phobia Workbook.* Oakland, CA: New Harbinger Publications, 1990.

Bunker, Linda J. "Golf: Sport Psychology Challenges," in *The Sport Psychologist's Handbook: A Guide for Sport-Specific Performance Enhancement,* edited by Joaquin Dosil, 301–320. West Sussex, England: John Wiley & Sons, 2006.

Chantal, Yves, Frederic Guay, Tzvetanka Dobreva-Martinova, and Robert J. Vallerand. "Motivation and Elite Performance: An Exploratory Investigation with Bulgarian Athletes." *International Journal of Sport Psychology* 27, no. 2 (1996): 173–182.

Cook, Kevin. "The Secrets of Tiger's Amazing Mind." *Golf Magazine* 50, no. 2 (June 2008): 88.

Cox, Richard H. *Sport Psychology Concepts and Application.* 2nd ed. Dubuque, IA: Wm. C. Brown, 1990.

Freeman, Criswell, ed. *The Golfer's Book of Wisdom.* Nashville: Walnut Grove Press, 1995.

Frost, Mark. *The Greatest Game Ever Played.* DVD. Directed by Bill Paxton. Burbank, CA: Walt Disney Studios, 1995.

Gauron, Eugene F. *Mental Training for Peak Performance.* Lansing, NY: Sport Science Associates, 1984.

Gill, Diane L. *Psychological Dynamics of Sport and Exercise.* 2nd ed. Champaign, IL: Human Kinetics, 2000.

Gould, Daniel. "Goal Setting for Peak Performance." In *Applied Sport Psychology,* edited by Jean M. Williams, 182–196. Mountain View, CA: Mayfield, 1998.

Hackett, Brendan. *Success from Within.* Limerick, Ireland: National Coaching & Training Centre, 1998.

Hall, Craig, Diane Mack, Allan Paivio, and Heather A. Hausenblas. "Imagery Use by Athletes: Development of the Sports Imagery Questionnaire." *International Journal of Sport Psychology,* 29 (January 1998): 73–89.

Haney, Hank. "Fix Your Pre-Shot Routine: Approach from Behind, Not the Side." *Golf Digest,* April 2008. golfdigest.com/instruction/longgame/consistency/haney_gd0804.

Hardy, Lew, Graham Jones, and Daniel Gould. *Understanding Psychological Preparation for Sport.* New York: John Wiley & Sons, 1996.

Harmon, Butch. "Swing to a Finish: One Simple Thought to Hitting It Fat." *Golf Digest,* July 2007. golfdigest.com/instruction/swing/2007/07/butchharmon_0707.

Horn, Thelma Sternberg, Curt Lox, and Francisco Labrador. "The Self-Fulfilling Prophecy Theory: When Coaches' Expectations Become Reality." In *Applied Sport Psychology*, edited by Jean M. Williams, 74–91. Mountain View, CA: Mayfield, 1998.

Jackson, Susan. A., and Mihaly Csikszentmihalyi. *Flow in Sports: The Keys to Optimal Experiences and Performance*. Champaign, IL: Human Kinetics, 1999.

Jacobsen, Peter. *Buried Lies*. New York: G. P. Putnam's Sons, 1993.

Jacobson, Edmund. *You Must Relax*. New York: Whittlesey House, 1934.

Jonesheirs Inc. "Bobby Jones," bobbyjones.com.

Khalid, Haythum R. "Famous Quotes About Visualization." famous-quotes.com/topic.php?tid=1278.

Kirschenbaum, Dan S. *Mind Matters: Seven Steps to Smarter Sport Performance*. New York: Cooper Publishing Group, 1997.

Kosslyn, Stephen M. *Image and the Brain: The Resolution of the Imagery Debate*. Cambridge, Massachusetts: MIT Press, 1996.

Landers, Daniel M., and Stephen H. Boutcher. "Arousal-Performance Relationships." In *Applied Sport Psychology*, edited by Jean M. Williams, 197–218. Mountain View, CA: Mayfield, 1998.

LeUnes, Arnold D., and Jack R. Nation. *Sport Psychology: An Introduction*, 2nd ed. Chicago: Nelson-Hall, 1996.

Locke, Edwin A., and Gary P. Latham. "The Application of Goal Setting in Sport." *Journal of Sport Psychology* 7, (1985): 205–222.

Martin, Kathleen A., and Craig R. Hall. "Using Mental Imagery to Enhance Instrinsic Motivation." *Journal of Sport & Exercise Psychology* 17, (1995): 54–67.

Miner, Mary Jane, Greg A. Shelley, and Keith P. Henschen. *Moving Toward Your Potential: The Athlete's Guide to Peak Performance*. 2nd ed. Farmington, UT: Performance Publications, 1995.

Morris, Tony, Michael Spittle, and Anthony P. Watt. *Imagery in Sport*. Champaign, IL: Human Kinetics, 2005.

Moulton, Amy. "Model Showing the Narrowing of Attentional Focus That Occurs with Increasing Mental Activation." Paper presented in Applications of Sport Psychology course, Ithaca, NY, 2001.

National Broadcasting Company. "Mental Games Trip up Athletes." January 26, 2006, nbcolympics.com/wesh/5088991/detail.html (accessed February 20, 2006).

National Broadcasting Company. "Tobias Angerer." nbcolympics.com/athletes/5091055/detail.html (accessed February 25, 2006).

National Broadcasting Company. "With Psychologist, Rocca Masters Mental Slalom." nbcolympics.com/alpine/5089926/detail.html (accessed February 21, 2006).

Nideffer, Robert M. *The Inner Athlete*. New York: Crowell, 1976.

Orlick, Terry. *Psyching for Sport: Mental Training for Athletes*. Champaign, IL: Leisure Press, 1986.

Orlick, Terry. *In Pursuit of Excellence.* 3rd ed. Champaign, IL: Human Kinetics, 2000.

Owens, Dede, and Linda K. Bunker. *Advanced Golf: Steps to Success.* Champaign, IL: Human Kinetics, 1992.

Parent, Joseph. "Zen Golf Lessons: The Best Golf You Can Imagine." *Golf Fitness,* (May–June 2008): 32.

Paivio, Allan. "Cognitive and Motivational Functions of Imagery in Human Performance." *Canadian Journal of Applied Sport Sciences* 4, (1985): 22S–28S.

Pearse, Wade. "Visualization for Golf—Feeling with Your Mind's Eye." golf-mental-game-coach.com/visualization.html.

Porter, Kay and Judy Foster. *Visual Athletics.* Dubuque, IA: Wm. C. Brown Publishers, 1989.

Quotes to Inspire You. "Imagination." Jack Nicklaus. cybernation.com/victory/quotations/subjects/quotes_imagination.html.

Reeve, Johnmarshall. *Understanding Motivation and Emotion,* 2nd ed. Fort Worth, TX: Harcourt Brace College, 1997.

Rendell, Jeff. "To Hit Straight, Play That Funk-y Music." *Washington Post,* May 5, 2006. washingtonpost.com/wp-dyn/content/article/2006/05/05/AR2006050500574.html.

Retton, Mary Lou. *Mary Lou Retton's Gateways to Happiness: Seven Ways to a More Peaceful, More Prosperous, More Satisfying Life.* New York: Broadway Books, 2000.

Rotella, Bob. "How Padraig Harrington Changed His Mental Approach and Won the British Open." *Golf Digest* 59, no. 6 (May 2008): 124–127.

Schempp, Paul and Peter Mattson. *Golf: Steps to Success.* Champaign, IL: Human Kinetics, 2005.

Schmid, Andrea, and Erik Peper. "Strategies for Training Concentration." In *Applied Sport Psychology,* edited by Jean M. Williams, 316–328. Mountain View, CA: Mayfield, 1998.

Shelley, Greg A. "Psychological Perspectives of Sport." Ithaca College, Ithaca, NY, 2000.

Sorenstam, Annika. "How I Track My Stats." *Golf Digest* 59, no. 6 (May 2008): 70.

Tschan, Manfred. "Motor Development and Skill Learning." George Fox University, Newberg, OR, 2000.

Wallach, Jeff. "The 15th Club." *Northwest Golf* 2, no. 1 (Spring 2008): 37–42.

Wann, Daniel L. *Sport Psychology.* Upper Saddle River, NJ: Prentice-Hall, 1997.

Weinberg, Robert. S, and Daniel Gould. *Foundations of Exercise and Sport Psychology,* 2nd ed. Champaign, IL: Human Kinetics, 1999.

Woodman, Tim and Lew Hardy. "Stress and Anxiety." In *Handbook of Sport Psychology,* 2nd ed., edited by Robert N. Singer, Heather A. Hausenblas, and Christopher Janelle, 290–318. New York: John Wiley & Sons, 2001.

Woods, Tiger. *How I Play Golf.* New York: Warner Books, 2001.

Yun, Hunki. "Lessons from Golf's Greatest Swing." *Golf Digest*, 1996. golfdigest.co.za/instruction/html/instruction3.php.

Zaichkowsky, Leonard D., and Amy Baltzell. "Arousal and Performance." In *Handbook of Sport Psychology*, 2nd ed., edited by Robert N. Singer, Heather A. Hausenblas, and Christopher Janelle, 319–339. New York: John Wiley & Sons, 2001.

Zinsser, Nate, Linda Bunker, and Jean M. Williams. "Cognitive Techniques for Building Confidence and Enhancing Performance." In *Applied Sport Psychology*, edited by Jean M. Williams, 270–295. Mountain View, CA: Mayfield, 1998.

INDEX

Erin Macy, M.S., earned a master of science in exercise and sport science, emphasizing in sport psychology at Ithaca College and a bachelor of science in athletic training from George Fox University (Newberg, OR). Upon completion of her degree, Macy worked as an academic advisor for student-athletes at Indiana State University and Southern Methodist University. Since her return to the Pacific Northwest, Macy has taught Mental Training for Athletes, an applied sport psychology course, at Portland Community College and worked at her alma mater, George Fox University.

Tiffany Wilding-White, M.S., is a sport psychology consultant to athletes in multiple sports from golf to figure skating, luge to soccer. A former national gymnastics champion, she knows firsthand the rigors of competitive athletics and the benefits of mental training. Wilding-White has worked as a mental skills coach for IMG Academies, including David Leadbetter Golf and Bollettieri Tennis in Bradenton, Florida, numerous private sports clubs, college and high school teams, and amateur and professional athletes. She holds a master's degree in exercise and sport science, emphasizing in sport psychology from Ithaca College and an undergraduate degree from Cornell University. With her husband, Carter, she lives next to a golf course in the Berkshire Hills of western Massachusetts. Visit her website at mindovermotion.com.